BABY
AN OWNER'S MANUAL

Bud Zukow, M.D.
and Nancy Sayles Kaneshiro

MJF BOOKS
NEW YORK

Published by MJF Books
Fine Communications
Two Lincoln Square
60 West 66th Street
New York, NY 10023

Baby: An Owner's Manual
Library of Congress Catalog Card Number 98-68233
ISBN 1-56731-312-4

This edition published by arrangement with Kensington Publishing Corp.

Manufactured in the United States of America on acid-free paper

MJF Books and the MJF colophon are trademarks of Fine Creative Media, Inc.

10 9 8 7 6 5 4 3 2 1

To my wife, Rozzi, for her love, patience, support, and especially her great humor. And to all my moms and my dads whose questions over the years have made this book possible.

BZ

To my husband, George, and my son, Ian, who are responsible for my greatest achievement . . . being called Mom.

NSK

ACKNOWLEDGMENTS

The authors would like to thank a few people who helped to make *BABY: An Owner's Manual* a reality. Thanks to agent—and cheerleader—Sandra Watt; Beth Lieberman, who bought the book over a tostada; Tracy Bernstein, our extraordinary editor (and new mom!) who babysat the manuscript along the way and improved it with every pencil mark she made; Charlie Hayward, who encouraged and advised—did everything *but* publish this book; and, finally, the authors would like to thank each other . . . they've known each other for thirty years or more, but this book has made them friends.

Dr. Bud Zukow and Nancy Sayles Kaneshiro

INTRODUCTION

Reading the Instructions

When your baby is first handed to you in the delivery room, be sure to remove the instruction booklet that is tied to his or her big toe. Guard these instructions carefully. These are the instructions that tell you everything you need to know about the care and feeding of a newborn, how to stop a baby from crying, how to have a rich and fulfilling life of your own while being a model parent. This is the only place you will ever find all the answers. *Warning:* Do *not* lose this instruction booklet! Doing so leaves even the most intelligent of new mothers wringing their hands in frustration without vital information needed not only for successful parenthood—but for *survival!*

Licensing and Qualifications

It has been said that there should be a license required for parenthood. After all, you need to take a road test in order to get a driver's license; you can't practice medicine, law, or accounting without a license; in fact, a business license is required for all business endeavors. Hell, you even need a license to go fishing! But to be a parent? One of the most difficult and important jobs in the world? This is left to the frightened, untrained masses, lacking in information, qualification, and trust in their own innate abilities. This is left to *you.*

And, what's more, nobody tells *anybody* that it's going to be a hard, hard job.

This book isn't going to make the job of parenting any easier. What it *will* do, however, is to help make the experience more rewarding, more joyful, by giving you some very specific information—some parenting "choices"—so that you may make informed decisions on how you will handle the wide variety of issues that crop up on a daily basis, decisions that will help you do the best for your child. We hope that somewhere during this dissemination of parenting pearls of wisdom, you will smile. But more importantly, we hope you will come to realize that no matter what you are experiencing in this most noble endeavor of parenthood, *you are not alone.*

BABY: An Owner's Manual is a book that is truly born out of necessity. No matter how many babies you've been around during your life, no matter how many books you've read, how much advice you've received, *nothing* prepares you for the thrilling, joyful, absolutely petrifying moment when you two get this new baby home and the door closes. There you are. The two of you. Alone. You and this baby. Oh, God.

In the hospital, the new mom has learned—hopefully—how to change a diaper on this little package who weighs less than last week's standing rib roast, what to do with a healing belly button, and, in about half the cases, circumcision, how feeding is accomplished—whether by bottle or breast—and that's about it. The rest, as they say, is sort of played by ear.

So, what does every new parent need? *Information.* An *owner's manual!* You wouldn't think of taking delivery on a new car without an owner's manual that tells you all about the workings of the car and manufacturer's suggested service intervals, would you? But a new baby? He or she arrives at home with a tiny diaper on its tush and virtually nothing else—no instruction book, no warranty, no service schedule, nothing to tell you *what to do!*

The truth is that nothing fully prepares you for that moment when mom or dad is first handed a brand spanking new infant. There is so much to know, so many issues that arise in the first moments, weeks, and months. These are the issues that *BABY: An Owner's Manual* will address.

It starts from the moment baby arrives at home. How do you get the baby on a schedule—before that little sucker puts you on *his* schedule? When can a baby sleep through the night? What about colic? Should we have a nurse? If so, what do we do when she leaves? Do we swaddle the baby? Should she sleep on her back? Her side? Her tummy? What *is* that on my perfect baby? *Diaper rash???* How much crying is too much? When should I call the doctor?

Whew—the baby is three months old and everyone has survived. So far. Now, what about mom going back to work? What about day care? How can mom care for her baby, work, take care of the house, pay attention to dad, and keep her eyes open past 8 P.M.? What if the baby—about whom you bragged shamelessly when he began to sleep through the night at five weeks—now wakes up twice in the middle of the night, *every* night? What about solid food? What are we ready for, and when?

And, are we having fun yet?

We *know* you're going to ask many of the questions we cover in the book because over the course of more than thirty years in pediatric practice, the questions have not changed!

Each stage of a child's life has its own issues to deal with. How often have we heard from "seasoned" parents that you only trade in one set of problems for another? *BABY: An Owner's Manual* addresses the first year or so of life and answers the questions that (a) parents have been too afraid or embarrassed or didn't know enough to ask, and (b) questions for which there is no single resource book in which to find the "answers," or suggestions, as we like to call them, since we all know that there really is no one "right" answer when it comes to raising children.

And that's what *BABY: An Owner's Manual* is really all about. Support, suggestions, tips, and most importantly *choices*—so that you may make informed, educated decisions to fit your lifestyle, your parenting style, your values—choices that are good for your children and good for you as well. A lot of what you will find in this book are very definite opinions regarding behavioral issues that have resulted from three decades in pediatrics. You are allowed to disagree with these opinions, and you are allowed to disagree with your own doctor. But do listen to your pediatrician on medical issues.

In fact, you'll find that "check with your doctor" is part of many of the answers in this book. Your doctor knows you, knows your baby, and is the best one to give specifics of treatment of illness and advice on feeding. One of our goals is to help you to create that all-important relationship with your pediatrician. That rapport will help you to be more secure and relaxed as a parent, and that will translate into a happier baby.

You have to give yourself time to develop a rapport with your pediatrician, and he or she has to give the time to develop one with the parent, too. Sometimes it doesn't happen for a long time—until something comes up outside of the routine "Here are the baby's shots, see you next month." A high fever, the flu, an ear infection, an injury—those things help you and the doctor find out what each other is all about.

In the meantime, find out about your doctor. Does she have a family? Does he work full-time? I've always felt that my patients should know as much about my personal life as I can share because I want them to know I'm as human as they are. I want to go away on vacation just like they do. You have to have respect for each other. You have to understand that pediatrics is the only specialty in medicine where the relationship lasts on this kind of continual basis. In no other field would a doctor routinely see a patient every month for the first year, four to five times the second year, and during the third year, you're into every earache and sore throat and you may be back to once a month.

If something happens in your family, go ahead and share it with the doctor. They want to know how your family is doing. No other specialty becomes a part of your life like pediatrics.

In *BABY: An Owner's Manual,* we're giving you some fast answers to questions we know you're going to ask, addressing the issues that are common to virtually all new parents. It is our aim that you realize that you are truly not alone in your feelings; that you understand that this is a tough job, especially in the first year when you're adjusting to the whole idea of parenthood; that you remember to laugh. That's why we've even tried to give you a chuckle or two along the way.

We hope you'll find *BABY: An Owner's Manual* user-friendly, and *parent*-friendly, for that was our intent.

Although we will touch on some medical issues along the way, we strongly advise that you add to your personal library a book that covers illness in children. Your pediatrician can recommend one for you, or you can peruse the ever-expanding parenting section in your local bookstore. This *owner's manual* is intended as an adjunct to your personal parenting library, as a source of easily accessible information that you have at your fingertips, one that you can grab in the middle of the night. It's intended to show that you as parents—and *your* feelings, *your* fears, *your* needs—weigh heavily in this complex equation known as a family.

First-time parents, and even second- and third-time parents, all cope with variations on essentially the same eating problems, sleeping problems, behavior problems, and relationship problems (between moms and dads as well as between parents and grandparents). Experience helps, patience helps, *sleep* helps, and the "perfect" baby would certainly help—but what really helps is recognizing that all of these problems are part of becoming a parent, part of a maturation process—yours and the baby's. We must grow as they grow. We must stay attuned to our needs as well as their needs—to be fed, held, loved with words and touch, talked to and talked with—and do all this while maintaining your own individuality and remembering that you were a *person* before you became a parent.

We are not born parents. We *become* parents and becoming is an endless process, a collection of experiences, questions, and answers. Although no one has all the answers, we hope that *BABY: An Owner's Manual* will give you a good, solid jumping-off point from which you embark on your own spectacular journey into parenthood.

Bon voyage!

Motherhood is so hard. How come nobody told me how hard it was going to be?

So, you're pregnant out to *there,* you're excited, you're apprehensive, you're retaining enough water to fill Lake Michigan, and you want to hear the *truth* about how motherhood is a round-the-clock job with lousy pay and virtually no vacation time? I don't *think* so! Besides, those who are in a position to tell you have probably forgotten all about those things in favor of the more joyful memories of new motherhood. And while it may be the hardest job in the world, the benefits are enormous.

The day my mother brought me home from the hospital, my father came home from work and found her sitting with me asleep in her arms, one shirt sleeve on and one off. "What are you doing?" he asked. "Well," she said, "I've been sitting here waiting for the baby to move his arm so I could put his shirt on." Nobody ever told her that it's okay to bend a kid's arm to finish dressing him. And the truth is that nobody tells *anybody* that it's going to be a hard job. You wouldn't really believe them anyway. You can't *know* until you've done it.

It's all happening so fast, my head is spinning. I'm "on call" day and night. Will I ever feel like myself again?

New parents must allow themselves a period of adjustment when undertaking the hardest job ever created. Although it is a job that brings with it great joy, it is a difficult 24-hour-a-day job, with a lot of anxiety and not much time off. This may sound funny, but the whole trick of adjusting to parenthood is to find out quickly how fast you can separate from the baby. This means going to a movie, out for a walk, or even going back to work.

You are dealing with the most dependent living thing in the universe, and you don't want to put yourself in the position of feeling that this baby can't be fed without you, can't be changed without you, can't be rocked to sleep without you. Learning this early will make the separation to day care, preschool, or kindergarten much less traumatic for both you and the baby.

How long should this adjustment take . . . really?

It takes as long as it takes. Some books say six weeks, some say three months. I say, *listen to your own body and your own emotions.* This is the most startling adjustment your body and your psyche will ever make, and regardless of what your mother, your neighbor, or your aunt Millie might say, you'll be ready for complete reentry into "real life" when you're ready. Period.

How do I know when I'm "adjusted"?

There are all kinds of "adjustments" when a new baby comes into your life. You are now living with a new human being, someone you don't know, and that's an adjustment. Your primary activity when you bring a new baby home is to take care of that baby—feeding, changing, bathing—this becomes your full-time "job," and for many new moms, this is an adjustment. Your relationship with the new dad changes instantly, since there is now someone else to consider, not just each other. This, too, is an adjustment. Add to all this the hormonal changes a new mother experiences, and a once happy, intelligent woman can feel (temporarily) as if she is a screaming maniac. The requisite fatigue that comes with motherhood doesn't help all of the above.

Each new mom "adjusts" in her own way and in her own time. Avoiding an artificial timetable and unrealistic expectations of her own feelings will help get new mothers back on an even keel more quickly.

Nobody's even shown me how to change a diaper!

Very soon, you will be an expert. You will do this in the dark, one-handed, in airplane seats, backseats of cars, restaurant booths, on your own lap. If you're in Southern California, add the tailgate of your four-wheel drive. You'll amaze your friends. You will be amazed at your own facility with this procedure. Meantime, after you remove a wet diaper, rinse the baby's bottom with a wet washcloth or with an unscented baby wipe. After soiled diapers, if you can, rinse the tush in warm water, or wipe thoroughly with an unscented baby wipe. Cleanse the genital area by wiping front to back. If you have a boy, carefully clean the scrotum. If you have a girl, make sure you clean the vaginal area—always front to back. With the new disposable diapers, putting a diaper on properly and getting a good fit is easier than ever before. And, a little practice goes a long way. There are, however, irrefutable laws of nature when it comes to diaper changing. As soon as you put a dry diaper on your little girl, she will wet it. And without a doubt, when you're changing your baby boy and you lean over him to coo and play, you'll get it in the eye.

Why do I have to go home from the hospital so soon? Why can't I stay an extra couple of days?

You have to go home because the insurance company says you have to go home And in the future, it's just going to be more and more that way. Although I am in no way opposed to cutting out excesses in medical treatment and hospitalization, perhaps allowing the insurance companies to call the shots as they are today is overcompensating . . . but that's another book.

Is sending new mothers home so soon dangerous?

I think the practice does carry a lot of risk. I believe it's unhealthy, and that it really doesn't give the mother a transition time from pregnancy to being a mother. It doesn't give anyone in the family that time. It certainly should be at least 48 hours. That gives a new parent the time to talk with the nurse and converse with the pediatrician. It's such a nice thing for the pediatrician to go in and chat with the mom and have an opportunity to answer questions before she and the baby go home.

#8 *How about for the baby?*

The baby will do just fine most of the time. However, the early release practice has, in fact, made it necessary for the pediatrician to see that mother and infant within the first 72 hours after they get home just to make sure all the parts work and there's no jaundice that should be cared for, and also to see that mom has an understanding of what to expect.

If I have a C-section, how long will I be in the hospital?

In most instances, three days at the most. Since this is considered major surgery, you will have to plan for a longer recuperation period at home. Most doctors want the mothers home for about two weeks after surgery and not behind the wheel of a car for three weeks.

#10 *In the case of a C-section birth, when do I bring the baby into the doctor's office?*

If the baby is not jaundiced when you leave the hospital, he should be seen at two weeks of age. Before you leave the hospital, ask the nurse if the baby is jaundiced. (See Question 11.)

What exactly is jaundice, anyway?

Jaundice is the name for the yellow that the skin turns from a buildup of the chemical called bilirubin. The bilirubin count is how we measure how jaundiced the baby is. A large percentage of babies get jaundiced, something my coauthor, Nancy, didn't know. After checking her baby at the hospital, I walked into Nancy's room and said, "Ian looks just fine, but he is a little yellow." She laughed and replied, "That may be so, but don't forget his dad is Japanese!" I almost fell off the chair.

#12 *Is jaundice dangerous?*

Jaundice is only dangerous if it lasts for a long time and if it's related to some kind of anatomical problem with the liver. Generally speaking, almost all jaundice is not anatomical but physiological, which means the liver cannot handle all the normal destruction of the large amount of red blood cells that come into the baby's body from the mother through the umbilical cord.

What's the treatment?

Jaundice is generally treated with ultraviolet lights, either at home or in the hospital. Since the baby's stay in the hospital is so short, the baby should be seen by the doctor at three, four, or five days of age to check for jaundice. Sometimes the baby requires home therapy. In some areas, there are groups of nurses who come to the house with lights and give treatments. Or your doctor may recommend putting the naked baby on a blanket in front of a window where the sun shines in directly for 10 minutes, three to four times a day.

#14 *How do you tell if the baby's better?*

Well, don't dress him in yellow clothing! Actually, your best bet is to lie the baby on a white towel or blanket in front of the window in natural light. That will give you a good idea if he is yellow or not.

#15 *Can I breast-feed if the baby is jaundiced?*

Sure. However, be aware that there is a controversy surrounding the opinion that a condition called breast-fed jaundice exists, in which the jaundice is prolonged because of breast-feeding. This is one of those theories about which you will hear various opinions, and those opinions should be respected. If your baby continues to be jaundiced, you might consider temporarily switching to the bottle.

#16 *Do you recommend having a baby nurse when we bring the baby home?*

I'm very much against it, and here's why. A nurse is paid for 24-hours-a-day work, so what she does is *work*—every time the baby cries, the nurse responds. In two weeks, when she's ready to leave, she says, "Here's your baby. He's wonderful!"

And you're so impressed to have a baby who was no trouble, the first time the kid cries, you don't know which end is up. To me, what a new parent needs in the house is someone who will take care of the house and cook a meal, because the parents are really exhausted. If there were somebody in the house at the beginning who could keep the house clean and cook the meals, it would make everybody's life easier . . . mom's, dad's, and the new baby's.

#17 *I've been told to put alcohol on the umbilical cord and Neosporin on the circumcision. Is this right?*

Yes, but don't do it in reverse because it's going to hurt like hell. Putting alcohol on the cord helps to dry it up. When it is totally dry, like a scab, it will fall off.

#18

After my baby shower, I could open a branch of FAO Schwartz. What first toys should my baby have?

I really think there's no such thing as too few toys. Ask the parents who've bought thousands of dollars worth of toys only to find the greatest pleasure the baby gets is when he discovers the Tupperware drawer in the kitchen. The first toys to give your baby should be something he can look at, brightly colored and moving; a small cuddly toy; or a squeezy toy that makes a little noise. In truth, a newborn doesn't need much. In my opinion, one of the best things to give the baby is a toy that plays him some nice music.

Like a musical mobile?

No! I am very much against any kind of mobile that hangs over a crib, because as the baby gets older, she may reach up and grab hold of it. If it breaks and pieces fall into her mouth, she could choke. So don't hang mobiles over a kid's head. It's just not a safe thing to do.

#20

My baby's belly button is bleeding a little bit. Is this serious? What should I do?

These days, babies are sent home so early—often 12 to 24 hours after birth—that the clip may still be attached to the cord. This clip will be removed by the pediatrician at a later date. A small amount of bleeding is nothing to worry about and may be caused by the baby's normal movements. Some newborn diapers have semicircles cut out so that the diaper doesn't rub on the cord. If your diapers don't have this feature, grab a pair of scissors and cut them out yourself! The bleeding will either stop by itself or can be stopped easily by applying direct pressure with a sterile piece of gauze. *Notify the pediatrician if the bleeding doesn't stop after 10 minutes of direct pressure.*

Why are well-baby checkups important?

Number one, they provide a health maintenance program for your baby. They also provide guidance for you as a parent and help you to develop a rapport with the physician who is going to care for your baby and be a part of your family for a long time. In addition, they help the pediatrician to gain an understanding of your family dynamics so that the doctor may be of real help to the family in times of stress.

#22 *Should my infant twins sleep together, or should I separate them so that they develop their individuality?*

Let them sleep together. I think it's terrific. They've been sleeping together for the past nine months, they can certainly sleep together when they first get home. As they get a little older, one may be more restless and the other more quiet. That's when they'll be more comfortable sleeping in separate cribs. But at the beginning, let them enjoy each other's company. It has nothing to do with their individuality. Twins, even identical twins, are no longer thought to be mirror images of one another. They are two children, each with her own distinct personality, talents, likes and dislikes.

#23 *My newborn keeps grabbing and pulling at his face. It looks like it must hurt. Is this normal?*

Sure it's normal. He finds his nose, he finds his ears, he finds his eyes. It's all part of the exploration process—coupled with the possibility that his skin may itch because it's dry. If his skin seems dry to you, put a drop of baby lotion on his face and smooth it in.

I'm worried that I'm not bonding enough with my baby.

If you are holding your baby lovingly, feeding him, bathing him, cooing and talking soothingly to him, you are automatically creating a *bond*—a closeness—with your baby.

But what's happening these days is that our society is getting hung up on the latest trends—on bonding, on breastfeeding, on absolutely everything from "save the whales" to "save the foreskins." We see it on every television talk show, we hear the "experts" talking about it and, as a nation, we react by going totally overboard without any regard to what is good for *us*.

The only thing the "experts" agree on is that we all want what is best for our babies. For my part, the most successful parents I have seen in 30 years of my pediatric practice are those who allow the baby to fit into *their* worlds from day one. These parents bond just fine with their kids, and are not plagued by what I see as *overbonding*, the '90s term for *spoiling*. These are the parents who wind up with a spoiled kid and a manipulative kid. It's important for new parents to get back into their routines as quickly as possible. Those who do are generally rewarded with more easygoing and independent kids as they grow.

I've handled lots of small children but never a newborn. What's the most important thing to remember?

Here are five:

1. Support the head.
2. Check the temperature of the bath water carefully.
3. Don't overdress the baby or overheat her room.
4. When holding the baby, don't do anything that isn't completely comfortable, like walk down a flight of stairs in the dark, or carry a sharp implement or hot coffee. Make sure there's nothing sticking out in the room that could hurt her head as you walk by. If the phone rings down the hall, put her down and go get the phone rather than run with the baby in your arms.
5. They won't break.

I feel under such pressure to breast-feed.

The La Leche League supports breast-feeding. Why not a *La Botella* League? Why not have people who promote bottle-feeding as easier, healthier, less time-consuming, and definitely quicker to get the newborn on schedule? Come on, it's unfair for anybody to make mom's choice. It strikes me as paradoxical that there are people who make breast-feeding almost a religion, and these are often the same people who say that women are in an era of choice. Some women are made to feel if they don't breast-feed, they're not being a complete mother, and there's just nothing further from the truth.

#27 *So, what's your take on breast-feeding?*

Breast-feeding is the most natural way for a mammal to feed its young. I have no problem acknowledging that it's good for the baby. I also have no problem telling you up front that it is *your* choice. It's your breast, it's your baby. Nobody has the right to tell you that you must breast-feed, nor should I or any other pediatrician or anyone tell you that you must bottle-feed.

Is breast-feeding going to give the baby the ability to go to college or be a good athlete? No. It has nothing to do with it. Breast-feeding is strictly for nourishment. It should be a choice, but in recent years, it's become a cult. A lot of pressure is put on the new mother to breast-feed and that's wrong. You get it from strangers, you get it from nurses in the hospital's nursery, and that's wrong.

#28 *What about bottle-feeding?*

I guarantee there are as many healthy babies raised on formula as there are raised on breast milk. I realize that the literature definitely indicates that breast-feeding is healthy, makes the babies strong, and gives them a natural immunity, and no one's going to disagree with that. However, if it doesn't work for you, for whatever reason—whether you're shy, or it hurts, or you don't want to—that's fine.

#29 *So is there a bottom line to this controversy?*

Dear Mom: They're your breasts. It's your baby. It's your choice. It's not La Leche League's choice, it's not your mother-in-law's choice, it's not your obstetrician's choice, it's not your pediatrician's choice, it's *your* choice. No one has the right to say otherwise.

#30 *Does breast-feeding hurt?*

Yes, sometimes it *does* hurt. Especially if you have a very hard sucker. The breast shield—a plastic device that pushes the aereola out—may help; so does pumping, because the pump is more gentle than the baby and allows the breast to heal and gives you a rest.

#31 *Can a breast-fed baby be supplemented with formula?*

Absolutely yes. There's nothing unhealthy about it at all.

#32 *The baby has been sleeping in a bassinet in our bedroom. Now what should we do? Put a crib in our room? In his room? In the hallway in between?*

You don't put the crib in your room. You don't put it in the hallway. So it's time to put it in the baby's room, which has been properly decorated, I'm sure. The reason you put her there is to make the initial separation—you from the baby, and the baby from you. If you want to keep the baby with you for a few weeks, that's up to you, but you should know that the baby will do fine in her own room from day one. And if the baby is with you for the first weeks, you'll wake up every time she makes a noise, or moves, or passes gas—and you really need all the rest you can get.

#33 *Should a newborn sleep in a bassinet or cradle instead of a crib because the size of a crib may be overwhelming?*

Not necessarily. There's nothing overwhelming for the baby about sleeping in a crib, though it might be a little overwhelming for the parents. The baby is going to scoot to the head of the crib or into one corner in order to be more comfortable and more secure. So feel free to use a crib from day one.

#34 *What do you think about demand feeding?*

I think demand feeding is the worst thing that was ever invented. It's the biggest imposition on parents that could possibly be. It means *you* have no time. If you think that a baby is hungry every time he cries, and you rush to feed him, you run the risk of creating a feeding problem. Just because a baby takes the breast, or takes the bottle and drinks two or three ounces every hour or two, doesn't mean he *needs* to. It just means the baby is responding to your offering him something. He loves your smell and the sound of your voice, and sucking comes naturally. The result is he's never quite full and never really empty.

Let's talk poop. My newborn poops several times a day. Is this normal?

You can figure a baby who is breast-fed is going to have about 1 1/2 bowel movements per feeding. And the same can be said for most formula-fed babies (it may be slightly less). After three months, a baby should have a bowel movement at least once a day, but it's not abnormal to go every other day, as long as his abdomen doesn't become distended, and he doesn't develop a colicky pain and constipation. And, on the other side of "normal," many babies poop after every feeding. Pooping after every meal, or during a meal, is okay—and rest assured this will end as soon as he is in school or preschool.

When the baby is a little older, I highly recommend a book entitled *Everybody Poops* (Taro Gomi, Kane Miller Book Publishers). Every parent and child should read it. I wish I had written it.

#36 *Should I be concerned if the color or consistency changes?*

Color and consistency are directly related to the diet. (My coauthor claims that strained carrots are exactly the same coming and going. I'm glad I never asked her to prove it.) It is also directly related to the age of the child. Changing a 4-week-old is a different experience from changing a 10-week-old. And the diapers of a breast-fed baby will differ from those of a formula-fed baby. As the baby gets older, she can develop constipation from something you eat, if you're breast-feeding, or something that she eats—constipating foods like banana, rice, or carrots. That will cause a harder stool and probably a change in color. On the other hand, a stomach flu, or consuming a lot of sugar or juice, may make the stool looser. If it continues for more than a day or two, or if it worsens in a short period of time, phone the doctor.

If the color should vary from red to purple to green, check the Play-Doh containers. No kidding.

If, however, the stool turns a very black-black, this is something that you will want to notify your pediatrician about right away. He will want to check out the baby for some potentially serious gastrointestinal problems.

#37 *Do I have to boil bottles to sterilize them?*

Absolutely not. I haven't told anybody to boil a bottle for more than 15 years. Dishwashers are great for baby bottles, but handwashing in hot soapy water is fine, too. If you do opt for the dishwasher, however, rinse the bottles in hot water afterward to wash off any soapy film that has stuck to them.

#38 *Are plastic bottles okay?*

Absolutely okay. You don't have to worry about dropping them and dealing with broken glass around an infant. And when the baby gets to be six or eight months old and begins throwing these things around, it hurts a lot less to be hit by a plastic bottle than by a glass bottle (both the thrower and the throwee).

#39

I hate to admit I'm afraid of this little bundle. She's so tiny, so fragile, I'm afraid she will break!

I've never seen a baby break—*ever*. Face it, you're going to handle her with kid gloves, as if she were the most expensive crystal in the world, because this baby is a miracle and because she's so new. She won't break. If you're afraid of the baby, it's only because you're a little unsure of yourself. Just know that this will change; in the second week, you'll have so much more confidence than the first week, and so much more at four weeks than at two. You'll really notice the difference when you have a second child and find you're just so much more at ease. You'll wonder why you were ever so afraid the first time around.

Is wearing nail polish okay? The baby puts my fingers into her mouth all the time.

I would imagine that it's pretty hard to get the nail polish onto those tiny nails, but if she'll sit still for it . . . Actually, as long as the polish is dry and your hands are clean, it's okay to put polished nails into a baby's mouth. It won't hurt her. But if she has teeth and/or your polish is starting to chip, don't do this. You don't want her to inadvertently ingest nail polish chips. Just use common sense.

Do I need to use boiled or bottled water to make formula?

Here in Los Angeles, before the 1994 earthquake, it had been 25 years since I had recommended boiling water for mixing formula. Then, due to possible contamination of the water supply, a great deal of chlorine was added to the system. Many parents then either used bottled water or boiled their water for formula.

So if you want to use bottled water, that's fine. There are also very good filtering systems available, whether it's one that attaches right to your faucet or purifies tap water that is poured through a filter into a pitcher. Otherwise, it really depends on your community and the source of water whether boiling is necessary.

Is it possible to spoil a brand new baby?

Over the years, many people have argued that point with me. I can recall one of my newer moms saying to me, "Dr. Zukow, I remember when Blakeley was three months old and you said to me, 'Put that baby down!' because all I did was hold her. But I didn't listen, and now she's really clingy. She doesn't like to play by herself. She always wants me with her." I use that story a lot when I'm asked this question, and the answer, of course, is a resounding "Yes!"

You can spoil them forever if you're not aware that you're spoiling. The loving attention you give with feedings, bathing, changing, talking or singing to her, taking her for walks or rides—this is enough attention for the infant. But *overresponding* to the baby, picking her up every single time she cries or whines, will lead to a spoiled baby and, eventually, a very frustrated parent.

Ask the parents the difference between how the second baby turns out as compared with the first when number one was a "consuming" child and number two got less attention because of all the time number one demanded. The second baby usually turns out more independent and more self-reliant and probably more easygoing. In the long run, life will probably be less stressful for the second one.

Should I interview a pediatrician before I make a choice?

Yes, I think it's very important to do so, and I urge you to interview more than one. What you're looking for is a pediatrician who is interested in answering your questions, a pediatrician who will spend as much time as possible, especially at the very beginning, being understanding and empathetic about your needs. I think it's important to find a pediatrician who has more than just the knowledge of how to treat a diaper rash or test for meningitis; the doctor you choose should be somebody who is a listener and a teacher. Based on these criteria, you make the selection. Choose very carefully. No other professional gets closer to a family for a longer period of time than a pediatrician.

Help! Hormones from hell have invaded my house!

No man, not even a male doctor who has dealt with thousands of pregnant and new mothers, can really know the extent to which the hormonal havoc wreaked by childbirth can affect an otherwise sane, happy, centered individual. Some new mothers find that even after hormonally triggered postpartum depression—or "baby-blues"—abates, she is still depressed.

Moms, there is another reason for depression at this stage . . . fatigue! I have found that the chronic fatigue factor that accompanies new parenthood often accounts for depression. The need to be "supermom of the century," juggling home, work, husband, and baby on four nonconsecutive hours of sleep per night would leave anyone a bit cranky. So I recommend the following: When the baby shuts his eyes, you lie down, shut off the phone, see no visitors, and sleep for an hour or two. With this method, you should be able to get about 8 hours during the course of any 24-hour period, and the fatigue and the depression should start to lift soon.

I am convinced that the fatigue syndrome that parents

often find themselves enmeshed in leads to not just being depressed during the first few months of parenthood, but increases the chances of becoming easily frustrated in many areas of life: your career, your relationship with your spouse, as well as with the growing challenges of parenting. So consider grabbing 40 winks a necessity, not a luxury. Dads—you, too. Create a family "rest time" when you get home from work. You'll be surprised how refreshing even a short snooze can be.

Is it okay for my three-year-old to see the baby at the hospital and be close to him right when he gets home?

Absolutely. He can even hold the baby—with supervision—so that no one gets dropped on his little head.

Is it obligatory that everyone who comes to see the baby gets to hold her, even if I'm not comfortable?

No—and for God's sake, don't feel guilty for saying no. This is *your* baby. You call the shots. So stop being nervous, but continue to be cautious. Whether or not to allow people to hold your baby is a personal decision. There are people who couldn't care less. I've even seen brand new babies passed around like footballs in our waiting room.

#47 *Yuck! Baby acne! My kid has teenage breakout and he's only four months old!*

Baby acne—yuck is right, but it's treatable. Use Dial Liquid Soap or any other antibacterial soap to help dry the outbreak along with a little Neosporin. Sometimes, just leaving it alone until it passes works just as well.

#48 *My newborn's eyes seem gunky. What can I do that won't hurt her eyes?*

It is possible that a newborn will develop "sticky eye," a mild infection caused by a foreign object getting into her eyes during delivery or a reaction to the erythromycin drops that are put into her eyes immediately after birth. The baby's eyes will ooze, and when she awakens, her eyelashes may be stuck together. Use a clean piece of cotton gauze to wash both eyes with warm water, starting on the inside corner and moving outward. Wash her eyes anytime you see they are sticky. If the sticky eye doesn't clear up within 24 hours or if you see any redness, call the doctor. Redness may indicate conjunctivitis, or pinkeye, which is very contagious, and the doctor will want to treat immediately with antibiotic drops.

I could swear the baby is looking in two directions at once, and it's creepy. Is this permanent?

For the first 8 to 10 weeks, it's normal for a baby's eyes to move in different directions, independently of each other. By about 3 months, however, his eyes should be permanently aligned. If they're not, bring it to the attention of the pediatrician so that the baby can be checked for strabismus, or crossed eyes. There are a variety of treatments for crossed eyes when the child is a bit older, ranging from exercises to glasses to surgery.

Also, the fact that there is no bridge to the nose in newborns and there are deep epicanthic folds in the corners of the eyes, toward the nose, may give the impression the eyes are crossing when actually they're not.

#50 *My baby's navel sticks out. Can this cause any kind of damage? Should I cover it?*

No and no. If his belly button bulges when he cries, he may have an umbilical hernia. For many years, we used to tape them with cotton balls to apply pressure, but the only thing the tape did was to irritate the skin around it because it was constantly getting dirty and wet. Put your finger in the belly button; if you can feel a small round opening, that's an umbilical hernia. They're very common. Even though they may seem to bulge when he cries, crying does not make them any bigger or last any longer, and generally speaking, by the time the child is four or five years old, it will go away by itself. I'm sure your pediatrician will be keeping an eye on it along the way and will advise you as to the best course of action.

My baby has an umbilical hernia. Does that mean he will have an "outie"?

No. I see so few "outies" as kids grow up that it's safe to say that most belly buttons will turn out to be "innies."

#52 *Why is my newborn baby losing his hair?*

Many do lose their hair during the first few months. But don't worry, the baby won't look like Kojak for long. He'll start growing permanent hair immediately. He may, however, still have a bald patch from rubbing his head against his mattress, playpen, or infant seat. This bald spot should fill in once he starts sitting up. As he gets enough hair for you to groom, do it gently, because vigorous hairbrushing can also cause hair loss. Let the doctor know if there has been prolonged hair loss and no replacement growth.

Is it difficult keeping grandparents from making suggestions?

Yes, but here's the key. Respect and listen to their suggestions, but follow through only on those about which you agree. Although grandparents are often wonderful sources of "how-to" information, many of the things grandparents suggest might have worked with their children (meaning you or the baby's father) but might not work for your baby simply because the times have changed—and your lifestyles are different. So take into consideration what they say, and if you have specific questions, ask the pediatrician.

It's too cold, it's too hot. What temperature should the baby's room be kept at?

Not more than 72 to 74 degrees and not less than 68 degrees—about a degree or two warmer than is comfortable for most adults. If possible, get a room thermometer to eliminate the guesswork, since temperatures in a house often vary from room to room. One common error of new parents is to assume that because the baby is very small, he's going to freeze in a big, bad crib. He's not going to freeze. In fact, it's worse for him to be overheated.

How do you feel about swaddling babies?

Swaddling was probably done at the very beginning of mankind. It was an easy way to carry the baby around. When a baby is swaddled, her arms can't flail a lot, she's not restless and, therefore, may sleep better. It's okay to swaddle, but you have to be careful about how hot the room is. And remember: If you and the baby are dressed in a sweater in the morning, and you take your sweater off later in the day, chances are you should take the baby's sweater off as well.

In my parenting class, there were a lot of absolutes given about how we should handle our babies. Some I don't agree with, but these people are "experts."

In parenting, there are as many schools of thought as there are "experts." The key to successful parenting, in my opinion, is to listen to what the "experts" have to say, then make your own choices. The reason is that each parent and each child comes from a different time and a different gene pool, so not all advice pertains to everyone. You are absolutely allowed to disagree with the experts. In fact, I encourage you to do so.

The truth is, there are no experts. The experts are really the children. They're the ones who tell us what's working and what isn't. We can only try things that we think might work. Every child is different, every parent is different, every time of day is different. Consequently, I don't see how anybody can set up a whole bunch of rules. When I tell parents when to start their baby on solid food, it's because he *needs* it, not because he is a certain age. The American Academy of Pediatrics may not always agree with me, but they don't know the baby—I do. So there are no absolutes.

#57 *How can I be sure that the baby is getting enough to eat?*

Eating and sleeping are the two basic areas of childcare in which most new parents are totally unprepared. You want to make sure that the baby is getting enough to eat, so you interpret each time the baby cries as a sign of hunger. It's a very natural response—it just doesn't happen to be the case.

You see, when a baby cries, it simply means the baby has awakened. He may or may not be hungry, but if you feed him, he'll eat—and you feel you've done something good for him, so you do it again and again. What happens is that the baby is never quite full and never quite empty.

However, if you use some kind of feeding timetable right from the beginning until you really get your feet wet and know what you're doing, you'll find that in about a week your baby is on a schedule, and in a month or so, he can come off a night feeding. This is where your own family doctor or pediatrician comes in. Somebody has to lay out ground rules for you, but the ground rules have to fit *you.*

For healthy, full-term babies, my rule of thumb for new parents is as follows: *Don't let newborns go more than 4 hours during the day without eating, and try not to feed them any more often than every 2 1/2 to 3 hours.*

Remember, if your baby has any health problems or was born prematurely and underweight, he might need to be fed more often. Your doctor will help you determine what's right for you.

#58 Honestly, what is the normal amount of crying per day in a newborn?

Under three months, a baby may actually cry from one to three hours per day. And that's a baby without colic, without constipation, without anything that's making her distinctly uncomfortable. That amount of crying can really rattle some new parents, so it's important to know that it's absolutely normal.

What should I do if the baby's crying more than the normal amount?

Remember to consider the following:

If he has a cold and is crying incessantly, you need to worry about an earache.

Has the baby failed to have a bowel movement in four days? That's a discomfort cry.

Does the baby have a milk allergy or is he reacting to something mom has ingested and is giving the baby via the breast? Babies get indigestion, too.

Does the baby, if under three or four months old, have a distended abdomen during prolonged crying spells? That's colic.

Check with your pediatrician if the baby is going through a prolonged period of crying so that she can check for any of the above maladies, plus the possibility of a hernia or some other unseen problem that might be causing pain.

Some kids are just screamers. Some, on the other hand, are great sleepers. I remember a day when a new mom and dad brought the new baby in for her three-month checkup. "She sleeps so soundly," the dad said, "and we're worried that she doesn't hear well because we make so much noise and she doesn't respond." I slammed my hand down on the table, making a loud bang, and the baby's head popped up like a shot.

Once every six months I get a couple like them, and my hand hurts for a week.

I've heard about the nightmare of colic. That's something we'll just have to suffer through, right?

Colic is a condition that occurs when the baby has swallowed some air and gets a little air pocket in the stomach—gas—and cries some more and swallows more air. The more the baby cries, the worse it gets. In fact, some of these babies will arch their backs and go totally rigid, screaming from the pain. At about three months, colic is usually just about over because the baby's digestive system has sufficiently matured by that time. While I cannot get into specific medicinal recommendations here, *do* talk to your doctor. There are some over-the-counter medications that are not harmful to the baby, and there are some decaffeinated herb teas that may help. So there *is* something that can be done for colic. You don't just have to live with it for three months.

#61 *How do I take care of the baby's sensitive little face?*

It's important not to forget to wash the baby's face. Otherwise, the chemicals in the milk and food that the baby gets on his face, or spits up and gets on his face, can cause an irritating rash. Just use a *soft* washcloth in warm water to wash his face as often as necessary throughout the day, not just at bath time.

#62 *I'm breast-feeding and I find the baby is less and less satisfied with each feeding during the day. What should I do?*

You might consider supplementing breast-feeding with a bottle of pumped breast milk in the late afternoon when you're tired or when there's so much for you to do that the quality of the milk may not be the same as earlier in the day—and the baby's hungrier. (Although we would have to send the breast milk to the lab to scientifically determine if the quality is indeed different from other times of the day, I can report that over three decades the incidence of babies' late afternoon feeding dissatisfaction is too frequent to ignore.)

How exactly do I get the baby on a schedule?

No one says this is easy. First, let me make a point that I think bottle-fed babies are easier to get on a schedule than breast-fed babies. Either way, for you to make a schedule, you're going to have to listen to a certain amount of crying. And remember these things:

1. Don't let the newborn sleep more than four hours at a time, except between the hours of 11 P.M. and 6 A.M. If she gets off the schedule, wake her so that her day starts at the same time each morning.
2. A newborn who goes three hours between feedings, whether bottle- or breast-fed, is doing pretty well. If the baby is up in between feedings during the first three weeks, don't give her the breast or formula, give her water or sugar water or even one of the herb teas like chamomile.
3. After about three weeks, the baby can go more than three hours, if you don't run right in and pick her up when she starts to cry. You will then notice that she's

going three hours and ten minutes, three hours and fifteen minutes, and so on.

4. By the time the baby is two months old, she should be sleeping through the night and be on only five or six feedings a day. Remember that I define "night" as about 11 P.M. to 6 A.M., so you should no longer be watching the Late Late Show.

Is there a period when the baby needs to be fed more frequently?

A lot of supporters of breast-feeding believe that there are growth spurts, during which a baby needs to eat more, but I believe that all normal children with good nutrition are in continuous growth. I think many breast-feeding proponents use it as an excuse to say that you can feed the baby anytime you want. But what you're creating if you do this is a habit. The baby cries, you put a breast in his mouth, he's content, he goes to sleep. It has nothing to do with how much the baby is growing or how fast.

Anyway, if you feed more during a growth spurt, you'll have to feed continually for 17 or 18 years!

I've heard a lot about "failure to thrive," and I have a very tiny baby. Should I be concerned?

When it comes to your baby's nutritional needs, you should *always* be concerned and *never* hesitate to ask. If you are two healthy parents with a six- or seven-pound, breast-fed baby who gains a pound in the first two weeks but nothing in the following two or four weeks, she is certainly not getting enough milk/fluids. But if you switch the baby to formula and she begins to gain weight, what you perceived as "failure to thrive" is over.

However, *failure to thrive that is persistent can represent kidney disease, heart disease, or severe gastrointestinal problems.* So failure to thrive is a serious diagnosis, whereas poor weight gain may not truly be a failure to thrive, it may just be that the baby isn't getting enough nutrition, something we often see in breast-fed babies. This can occur at the very beginning if mom is not producing enough milk or if the milk is not of high quality. I believe not all breast milk is equal.

Should I have my son circumcised?

I recommend it. Circumcision is no longer just a religious rite. About 95 percent of my patients circumcise their little boys as a hygienic measure. The decision to circumcise is in the majority for health reasons, religious reasons, and because many parents are concerned that their boy look like the other kids or look like dad. But it's strictly up to you.

Who does the circumcision?

Most circumcisions are done either in the hospital almost immediately after birth (performed by the obstetrician who, generally speaking, is more capable of completing a hygienic, aesthetic circumcision), or at home in a Jewish ceremony called a *bris* at eight days of age (performed by a *mohel,* a religious figure who is also responsible for giving the baby his Hebrew name and welcoming him into the Jewish community).

#68 *Does it hurt?*

Yes. But we all survive. All of the babies and most of the mothers.

#69 *Does it cause trauma later in life?*

In my opinion, the answer is no.

#70 *I had my son circumcised in the hospital, but now that I'm home, I'm not sure how to care for him. Any tips? (Ha!)*

There really are very few problems associated with circumcision. But these days, infants are usually home from the hospital in about 24 hours, so instead of trained nurses being available to observe if there's any excess bleeding, you're going to have to do the observation at home. Circumcisions heal very well, usually in five to six days.

A *tip?* Place a small piece of gauze dabbed with Vaseline

or, preferably, Neosporin over the penis so the diaper doesn't stick to it. Use new gauze with every diaper change. Another *tip?* Cut up the little gauze squares in advance so that you're not handling a scissors while you're changing the baby.

#71 *Is a vaginal discharge normal in newborn girls?*

Yes, there will be a slight discharge and it may even be slightly bloody. It's nothing to worry about. It's just a result of having the mother's hormones still going through her system. It should go away by the end of the first month.

#72 *I thought my new baby was just a little chubby, but she actually seems to have little budding breasts. Is this possible?*

Yes. Little girls *and* little boys may have some slight breast engorgement—and maybe even a little secretion—after they're born, and this, too, is because of mom's hormones left over in the body. This may last anywhere from two to six months.

#73

Does a new baby need a bath every single day? I don't want her skin to dry out.

I certainly think she does. Babies, because they spit up, because they poop, because they pee—and these are the three most important things they do—sometimes smell really bad. And babies can smell really nice! If you use very mild baby soap and shampoo on the baby, her skin isn't going to dry out. Plus, there are lots of wonderful nonoily lotions on the market you can put on the baby to keep her skin soft and moist (but make sure she doesn't slide right out of your hands when you pick her up!).

#74

Where should I bathe the baby?

Newborns can be bathed anywhere: the kitchen sink, the bathroom sink, or even in the bathtub if you use a baby bath. Here are a few things to remember:

1. TEST THE WATER TEMPERATURE before you even pick the baby up to bring him to the bath.
2. Hold him in the bath by supporting his head with your hand.

3. Squeeze a little baby soap over the baby and rub lightly with a baby washcloth.
4. Wash *everywhere.* Babies have folds and creases in the oddest places. I've even seen babies with creases in their creases! (Check in between those tiny toes!)
5. Don't take your eyes off this baby for even one second. They are *fast!*
6. Wherever you decide to bathe him, make sure those little hands can't inadvertently grab the hot water handle. When you're playing with the baby, cooing at him, that's when accidents happen. Babies are accidentally burned in the bath more than anywhere else.

Yuck! What's this scaly yellow crust on my beautiful baby's head?

Ah yes, the heartbreak of cradle cap! Some people call it "cradle crap," and I think that's a pretty good name for it, too. The medical term for it is seborrhea, which means "oily scalp." Use Fostex soap as a shampoo and then do a Vaseline massage with your fingernails to loosen the stuff. Wipe it off with a washcloth. You might have to do this for five or six days in a row, but that should do it.

#76 *I'm so paranoid about SIDS, I run in 100 times a day to see if he's still breathing.*

I always tell new parents that for the first three or four days, when the baby's quiet, they're going to be in the baby's room; when the baby's crying, they're going to be in the baby's room. At the end of the fourth day, they'll find they've never left the baby's room! But remember, you can't begin your life as parents thinking that something horrible is going to happen. For your own sanity and for the baby's well-being, you've got to believe that your baby is going to be just fine. The truth is that we don't really know too much about the cause of sudden infant death syndrome (SIDS), but we can make sure our babies are comfortable and safe. Keep the following in mind:

The safest way for the baby to sleep is on his stomach. If you put him on his back and he spits up, there's no way he's going to be able to get his head out of the way and prevent himself from choking. (Once he's old enough to roll over, his head will be strong enough to get out of the way if he spits up.) To avoid the danger of suffocation, put the baby on something firm, with no pillow. The most comfortable way for a baby to sleep is on his stomach. Babies are much less restless when they're on their stomachs (see Question 92).

#77 *Are sideboards necessary for sleeping?*

Only if you feel insecure about the infant being on her stomach. Once the baby can move around a bit, the sideboards will not keep her from turning onto her stomach anyway. When babies lie on their stomachs, there's less flailing of their arms and legs, they're more comfortable, and they can get into their fetal position a lot easier than when they're propped up on their sides. But some people in the baby products business saw sideboards as a new industry, and now they even have designer sideboards.

#78 *What do I put on her tush to clear up this awful diaper rash?*

There are a million remedies for diaper rash on the market, and I guess each pediatrician has his favorites. In our office, we've discovered that if you mix two over-the-counter medications, Neosporin and hydrocortisone cream, you get a mix that approximates an expensive pharmaceutical remedy containing an antibacterial and an anti-inflammatory. Put a little of each on your forefinger, mix it together with your thumb and forefinger, and apply to her tush. This should take care of the rash right away. However, if it's a yeast infection, you'll need a prescription for a medicated powder and cream. (See Questions 81 and 82 for more on yeast infections.)

#79 *Is there any way to prevent diaper rash?*

Since this is an area with such a great deal of traffic, try to keep the baby as clean and dry as you can, changing his diaper as frequently as possible. There are a number of products on the market that you can use to protect the skin. Personally, I like A&D ointment. It is the least offensive of the diaper rash remedies/preventatives and at least your baby won't smell like fish.

Can I use baby wipes on a newborn?

Sure, as long as they're unscented. Perfumed wipes can cause diaper rash, and since there's so much going on in that area, you can be sure that anything that *might* encourage diaper rash will succeed.

#81 *Yikes! A yeast infection! What do I do?*

Your pediatrician will no doubt have her own favorite remedy for yeast infections, but remember this: Do not use cornstarch. It's food for the yeast. A yeast infection is a heavy, angry, red, fairly well-delineated rash, with satellite red dots, that will not respond to the normal kind of ointments you may try for diaper rash—A&D, for example. The prescription you will need is for Mycolog cream and Mycostatin powder, which when combined is an antifungal treatment.

#82 *How in the world could my baby get one?*

Yeast infections can be picked up from the air. Also, as a baby gets older he urinates less frequently so the urine is more concentrated and acidic, which may contribute to a yeast infection. Sometimes the baby will have white patches, called thrush, inside his mouth. (See Question 105.) The infections go through the gut and come out in the laundry, and the baby could wind up with a yeast infection in the diaper area.

#83 *How important is it to insist on a particular bedtime?*

Bedtime is *your* time as parents. If you don't care that the baby goes to sleep at a different time every night, that's fine. That's your choice. But for parents who need their rest and who have so little time to spend together, I think it's very important to establish a bedtime, and this you can do from day one.

What if the baby isn't tired?

Sleep patterns are created by habit. Once the baby gets into the habit of sleeping at certain times, the bedtime you establish will be *his* bedtime, too.

My husband thinks it's cute when the baby sleeps with us. I don't think it's so damn cute!

I answered that one just the other night. Usually, a parent will suggest this because allowing the baby to sleep with you eliminates the need to walk a crying baby. It's an easy way out and, unfortunately, a rather addictive habit that is going be increasingly difficult to break, if this practice continues.

When can the new baby be taken out?

I've seen such small babies in strollers at shopping malls, I'd swear they were born in the parking lot. While I am in favor of active mothers, I don't think a newborn has any business out and about for the first three weeks, with the exception of a trip to the doctor.

#87

Should I be concerned about small children getting near the baby?

Yes. However, if the baby has an older sibling, there's not much you can do to prevent contact. I've always told parents that the rule of thumb is if the oncoming child in the mall or in the park isn't taller than your kneecap, you can count on him carrying some kind of infection. So keep a little distance.

#88

With a new baby in the house, I'm not sure what's safe to clean with. What do you suggest?

A disinfectant cleaner, like Lysol, appropriately diluted, will not hurt the baby—unless he drinks it. Once your baby is crawling, your whole way of cleaning will change, because your house will never really be "clean" all at once again. You'll be cleaning the kitchen floor where he threw up, and he'll be in the living room, making some other kind of mess. The trick is not to let it make you a nervous wreck.

My mother-in-law is turning my house into an operating room. She wants everything sterile . . . "for the baby."

As a doctor, I really can't complain about someone insisting on cleanliness around a new baby. However, I don't think it's necessary to sterilize a newborn's surroundings. I'd rather have the child in a nice, clean environment that is kept that way on an ongoing basis than in a germ-free bubble for two weeks when Grandma is visiting. Also, watch what she's cleaning with. You don't want the baby around any fumes that might be dangerous to her tiny respiratory system.

She also insists that everyone wash their hands before touching the baby.

Again, I can't go on record against handwashing. In fact, it's really not a terrible idea. Even for people who are meticulous about washing their hands after they use the bathroom, you can be sure that before they arrive at your house, they've touched dozens of doorknobs and handled money, for example, so a quick wash of the hands is not a bad thing.

But that's only part of the issue here. Who's calling the shots in your house? You or your mother-in-law? However well intentioned—and often *right*—she is, it's best from the start to establish your own territory with regard to this baby. You are, after all, the parent.

#91 *When is the baby old enough to leave with a baby-sitter?*

As the parent advocate that I am, I would say right away—as soon as you feel well enough to be up and around. A week, maybe. If you had a C-section, and your doctor wants you to be home for two weeks, my answer would be two weeks. I think it's good for you, and the baby, for you to get out just as soon as possible. I think the longer you wait, the harder it is to make the separation. Get a trusted relative to watch the baby for an hour while you escape for a cup of coffee, and you will find that even a brief respite is refreshing. There is no hard and fast rule here, just good common sense.

Of course, whenever you leave a baby with *anybody,* make sure they know where you are, they know enough English to use 911, and they have easy access to the name and telephone number of the pediatrician.

#92 *Should my baby sleep on her stomach, side, or back?*

This certainly ranks as one of the most frequently asked questions I get from new parents. And I always answer this way: The American Academy of Pediatrics has come out with the recommendation that although we have put babies on their stomachs for generations, now they should sleep on their backs or sides.

I will not recommend that a baby sleep on her back until someone will take responsibility for when that child spits up and chokes. Period. Sleeping on their sides is fine. Stomach-sleeping is also perfectly acceptable as long as it is without a pillow and on a firm enough mattress so that the baby's nose and mouth cannot be pushed into it. From my point of view, this is not negotiable.

#93 *I think my older child invented sibling rivalry. I expected some jealousy when the baby was born, but nothing like this.*

When a new baby is brought into the home, the older sibling usually wants his parents to take it back. He would like to put it in a nice package and give it to somebody else. I recently saw a newborn in the office whose older sister is six years old. She said, "If Zack and I don't get along, would you take him home?" She meant it, too.

"You'll get along," I told her.

"Well, we're not," she replied with righteous indignation.

I think the best analogy I've ever heard was when I participated in a panel discussion on parenting many years ago. A lady in the audience asked, "What do I do with my five-year-old boy when I come home with a new baby?" Without hesitation, a psychiatrist who was also on the panel said, "Can you imagine that after you come home from the hospital, your husband comes home in the middle of the day with a young lady on his arm and says, 'Hi, this is Loretta. She'll be living with us for a little while. She won't interfere with anything, and you'll just continue to do the cooking and cleaning and the usual stuff. You'll be okay with that, right?' To me, it's the same thing."

After all, how do you expect a kid to say, "It's wonderful. I can share my mom and dad now with this little lump who does nothing, and everybody waits on him . . . and *I* should be potty trained? This kid gets his tush wiped 14 times a day, and I have to do it myself!"

The older a child is, the busier he is with friends, school, or other activities and the quicker he's likely to adjust to the new baby. In the meantime, the attention he gets from you shouldn't be any less or more than before the baby.

#94 I've heard jealousy makes older brothers and sisters revert to babyhood.

I don't believe kids have an innate understanding of jealousy. I really don't. I do believe, however, that when you bring a baby into a house with a toddler, he knows that now he has *competition.* He knows he can't use you all the time, that sometimes you're busy. So he throws tantrums, he throws food, he wets his pants, he does anything to get your attention. It's also fairly common for a toddler to want to revert to drinking from a bottle or even to breast-feed. Both should be discouraged. Rest assured this will pass, especially after he is in nursery school or elementary school full-time. That's where he has his own society, his own friends, his own things to do.

#95 What should I know about a newborn with a fever?

Warning to all parents, grandparents, baby-sitters, and other caregivers of newborns:

Within the first month, any temperature above normal, whether associated with other symptoms or not, should be answered by a call to the physician. *Do not delay!*

If the baby is one to three months old and has a temperature of 102 degrees or higher that is accompanied by a lack of appetite, call your doctor immediately. If she has a fever accompanied by vomiting or diarrhea, call your doctor immediately.

Although an elevated temperature may not mean anything in and of itself, other symptoms, such as lack of appetite, lethargy, or dull eyes, make even a low-grade fever such as 100.6 and above significant. The doctor's main concern will be treating any serious infection that may be present and keeping the baby from getting dehydrated.

#96 *What is a normal temperature?*

Normal temperature for an infant, taken rectally, is 99 to 99.8 degrees. It will differ if taken other ways.

#97 *What is the best way to take a temperature?*

You may not want to hear this, but the answer is *rectally*. That's the most accurate temperature there is. Any nurse in any doctor's office will tell you that.

#98 *What about those new ear-scan thermometers?*

They're wonderful, if used correctly. But sometimes babies' ear canals are so small, it's a very difficult procedure to accomplish without a lot of practice. Our nurses, of course, get an awful lot of practice, but new moms don't have that experience and often have a great deal of trouble getting an accurate reading. That leads to two potential problems. Either you run to the doctor for an unnecessary office visit, or you don't come in when the indications are indeed there. So rectal is still better.

#99 *Have you ever run across another new parent who felt as totally unprepared as I do for this enormous task?*

Are you kidding?

Two of my favorite stories about the unpreparedness of new parents come from very bright, educated young ladies. One is an adoptive parent who said: "I was so unprepared. I didn't want to read anything or buy anything or get too excited every time we thought we might be getting a baby, just in case it didn't work out that time. So when the day finally arrived and I came home with my daughter, she was wrapped in the one and only receiving blanket we owned, and she spit up on that in the car on the way home!"

That was only topped by another young mom who said she was afraid to give the baby a bath. She pored over pictures in a baby book for hours on end before she finally got up the nerve to submerge the baby in a sinkful of water. When I told her that was a normal reaction for new mothers to have, she said, "Yes, but she was *three weeks old* before we got her wet!"

Isn't it true that if the baby takes a bottle, he won't want to breast-feed anymore?

I don't think there's any truth to the premise that if the baby gets hold of a rubber nipple, he won't want your nipple, because if a baby starts off that way from the beginning, he'll quickly get used to the combination. This is especially important for the working mom who can't be home all day to feed and for the dad who wants to participate in feeding the baby. And it helps a great deal when it comes time to wean the baby. The longer you wait, the more difficult it is for the baby to adjust to the rubber nipple.

#101 *My newborn has a rash on her cheeks that seems to worsen after a feeding. Could she be allergic to me?*

Could be, but more likely the chemicals in the milk collected on her face when she spit up and have irritated her skin. Wash her face with tepid water after feeding, dry gently but thoroughly, apply a little lotion, and the rash should disappear.

Can his umbilical cord come untied?

I have this vision of an umbilical cord coming untied and a baby flying around the room backward, deflating like a balloon! Actually, an umbilical cord itself is not tied. It is either clamped or tied off with a tie that falls off when the cord heals, but the cord itself is not tied in a knot. If the cord bleeds a little, a little pressure should stop the bleeding within a very few minutes. If the cord doesn't stop bleeding after about 10 minutes of pressure, give the doctor a call.

#103 *I'm not sure I want my baby to use a pacifier, but it makes going to a restaurant or a movie so much easier.*

I swear I think my waiting room looks like the "March of the Binkie Brigade." I'm convinced that the recent increase in the use of pacifiers is a direct result of our reaction, once again, to the latest trends. It is currently trendy to think that a baby needs to suck all the time. (It is also profitable to spread this belief, especially if you are the manufacturer of designer "binkies.") I would like to ask all the people who are recommending pacifiers if *they* had pacifiers when they were young, and if not, how did they ever succeed in life without satisfying this great sucking need? (And after all, the baby doesn't really belong in a restaurant or movie theater. You'll enjoy yourself more—and get a needed break—if you leave him with a baby-sitter.)

Using a pacifier creates an addiction that the baby doesn't get by choice. If the baby puts his thumb in his mouth, that's his choice. If we put a pacifier in his mouth, we're forcing the baby to do something. Secondly, most parents get accustomed to sticking a pacifier in the infant's mouth anytime he makes a noise. Remember that it's normal for kids to "talk" to themselves, making squealing noises, crying noises, and sucking noises. When you see a three-year-old with a blue pacifier hanging around his neck and a red one in his mouth to match his outfit, that's a kid who can't break the habit. And, it doesn't allow the kid to talk. I swear to you, I have three-year-olds in my office who, when you ask them a question, try to answer through a pacifier. It's just better not to get started with them in the first place.

#104 *Isn't thumb-sucking the same thing?*

Revelation! There's nothing wrong with thumb-sucking! I always tell parents that their children will quit sucking their thumbs by the time they graduate from high school. Want proof? Take a look at your friends. While they may have a lot of other questionable habits, hardly a one is sucking his thumb!

Seriously, since most children give up thumb-sucking on their own, why fight it? A pacifier is not a substitute for thumb-sucking.

#105 *There's some cheesy stuff in her mouth, and I can't get rid of it.*

If you're looking at white patches that coat the inside of her mouth and her tongue and cannot be wiped off, you're looking at a condition called thrush. Thrush is caused by a yeast called *Candida* that grows rapidly on the lining of the mouth. It affects areas that are rubbed against by continual sucking. In addition to breast-feeding, this condition may be prolonged by allowing a baby to sleep with a bottle in her mouth or by a large pacifier. It's not contagious and can be controlled with a drug your doctor can prescribe called nystatin oral suspension.

Place the nystatin in the front of the mouth on each side (it doesn't do any good once it's swallowed). If the patches don't start improving in two days, rub the nystatin directly on the patches with a cotton swab. Keep this up until all the thrush has been gone for three days.

Can she nurse if she has thrush?

Yes, but reduce the time she feeds to a maximum of 20 minutes, because with thrush, it's sometimes painful for her to suck.

Often we recommend treating the thrush and discontinuing breast-feeding for about 48 hours until the thrush is better, so that the condition isn't passed back and forth between mother and baby. Give the baby a bottle for a couple of days, but remember to wash the nipple thoroughly after each use and avoid giving the same nipple back to the baby feeding after feeding. It's easier to get thrush off a rubber nipple in a dishwasher than it is to thoroughly remove it from the breast.

#107 *It hurts her to suck, but she's hooked on a pacifier. I have a very unhappy camper here.*

First, sterilize the pacifier. Limit the use of the pacifier, except when it's needed for going to sleep. Consider this a great time to wean her off of the pacifier and get rid of it altogether.

#108 *My infant screams with each bowel movement, and I think I saw a little blood in his diaper. I am panicked!*

Don't panic. This is probably due to an anal fissure, a small tear or crack in the skin at the opening of the anus. More than 90 percent of children with a few streaks of bright red blood after a hard bowel movement have an anal fissure. Constipation is the usual cause.

What's the course of action?

The bleeding from an anal fissure usually stops on its own immediately after the bowel movement. To heal the fissure, give the baby warm baths, three times a day, but don't use any soap on the irritated area. If the baby is on solid food, increase the fruits, vegetables, and bran products to help make sure the stool is soft; decrease milk products and avoid rice. Occasionally a stool softener may be needed temporarily. You may use a combination of Neosporin and cortisone cream on the crack to help the healing process. Call the doctor's office if the fissure isn't completely healed in three or four days or if the bleeding recurs.

My newborn has a white tongue and it won't go away. What is this?

If the baby has no other symptoms, like cheesy patches on the inside of her cheeks, she just has a little "milk tongue." Not to worry.

My environmental conscience has me leaning toward cloth diapers. Convenience has me clipping Huggies' coupons. Any opinion?

Very definitely. There's no question that the disposable diapers are better. You get much fewer and milder diaper rash problems. The only problem we see with disposables is that they absorb so much liquid, you often can't determine if a child is dehydrated by checking the wetness of his diapers. Sometimes you can't tell if he's wetting at all.

Another disadvantage of cloth diapers is that you have to soak the poopy ones—often in the toilet for convenience. On a busy night, you can occupy every toilet in the house before the night's over!

How do I choose a good baby-sitter?

Again, this is where good common sense, and your own sense of comfort, will come into play. First of all, you have to have a lot of confidence in that person. It should be somebody who has experience with infants, and once again, somebody who is able to converse with 911 and the doctor's office. You have to understand that the baby isn't going to be taken care of as well as *you* can do it. That's a given. The most important part is that you're getting out.

That's going to make you a more relaxed parent when you get home.

Fortunately, the babies—and almost all of the parents—survive the experience. The first time, you really do have to wean yourself. Just go out for that cup of coffee, so that you can be home in an hour and reassure yourself that the baby is still okay. Then, the next time, go out for a couple of hours. Build up to dinner and a movie.

Isn't it better to be a mom who stays at home with her kids all day?

It's terrific if you can afford to be a stay-at-home mom in this day and age. Statistics show that not too many women can stay home and be full-time mothers. But remember one thing. Very soon that baby will be going to school six hours a day. Both of you need to be prepared for that degree of separation. I think day care is a very good way to start.

#114 *Choose day care over all day with mom?*

You bet. Most modern mothers that I know appreciate their children so much more when they are not with them 24 hours a day, seven days a week. Day care affords the mother time to work, time to tend the house, time for herself (pick one, not all three!). Also, day care is very important for socializing the kids and getting them ready for the big separation when it's time for nursery school.

One mom whose child had been in day care since he was about five months old told me, "You know, on the first day of preschool, there was an awful lot of crying, kicking, and carrying on. But I finally pulled myself together and went home!"

How much should a newborn be awake?

What you hope is that your newborn will be awake for feedings and to sit on your lap and smile at you and then go back to sleep. Even if that happens, which it often doesn't, the baby will be awake an *aggregate* four to five hours a day. While that doesn't sound like much time, remember that it is all in little chunks, every three to four hours, around the clock, and that's why you're exhausted!

#116 *How many hours at three months?*

A third of a day. They should be awake about eight hours in any 24-hour period and should be starting to give you longer nights, edging toward that ideal of 11 P.M. to 6 A.M. time frame.

At six months?

At six months, they're up nearly half a day, about 12 hours, which makes it a *looooong* day. And it's up to you to shorten that day if you need to by scheduling naps or periods when they are awake but away from you (such as in the crib or playpen) and playing by themselves.

#118 *Why does my baby drool so much?*

An infant begins to drool at about two months and drools until all of her teeth are in. A significant percentage continue to drool, especially kids with any kind of nasal obstruction or allergy. Some babies are just bigger droolers than others. While most people associate drooling with teething, the fact of the matter is that the salivary glands are producing as much saliva as adults have—and it has to go somewhere!

#119 *How long should a baby breast-feed at one sitting?*

I think 30 to 40 minutes is ideal. Most women switch the baby to the other breast halfway through, but you can also breast-feed only on one side, alternating with each feeding.

#120 *Should a bottle-fed baby always finish the bottle, no matter how long it takes?*

No. Again, I think a limit of 30 to 40 minutes should be set right away. That's a lot of time to spend feeding. Multiply that over seven or eight feedings a day, and you can be spending upward of four or five hours a day just feeding. If the baby's snoozing during a feeding, or playing, you're stuck for another couple of hours. It's just not necessary.

#121 *How do you know when to burp the baby?*

Give it a try after a couple of ounces. (With a newborn who might only be taking two ounces, try after about one.) Some babies will burp more, some less. If you have a good "latcher," whose mouth tightens around the nipple, he will swallow less air and burp less than other more "loose-lipped" babies.

#122 *What's the best way to burp the baby?*

The three most popular ways to burp the baby are:

1. Sit him up on your lap, lean him over slightly, supporting his chest with one hand, and pat his back with the other;
2. Lie him across your lap, facedown, and pat his back;
3. Put him up on your shoulder and *gently* pat his back, or,
4. When he's up on your shoulder, rub his back, gently pushing from bottom to top.

You'll no doubt find one that is most comfortable for you . . . or use a combination of all of the above.

Do breast-fed babies need to be burped?

Yes, but they tend to swallow less air than bottle-fed babies, and, therefore, will burp less.

#124 *I try and try and sometimes I just can't get her to burp. Is that okay?*

If you try to burp the baby and she doesn't burp, sure that's okay. She just doesn't have to burp.

Is there an age when babies no longer need to be burped?

Yes, when they look at you sweetly and burp in your face—all by themselves. They think it's such a great accomplishment. This usually happens once they've started to sit up and/or crawl, about six months old. By the time they're four, you'll be sorry they ever learned!

How do I choose a day-care facility?

Check references. Ask questions. Visit on an impromptu basis. And if there is any objection to any of these things, move on. I always suggest that parents get recommendations from other parents who have already had their kids in day care. Or get a recommendation from your pediatrician's office. Also, many churches and synagogues offer day care and that, too, might be a good place to start.

When you visit, you will have a gut reaction whether or not this is the place for your baby. Take a look at how the other babies there are being handled. Are they held while being fed? Talked to lovingly? Are they taken outside when weather permits? Are they being kept clean? Let your nose tell you if diapers are being changed at appropriate intervals. And ask a million questions if you need to. You'll know when you've found the right place for you.

#127 *My baby seems so much smaller than others her age. Should I be concerned?*

I know a mother who's barely 5´ tall and a father who's 5´1˝, and they want their child to be 6´2˝. I asked them if anyone in the family has ever been over 5´8˝ and they said no—I had to tell them that they'd better find a different way to measure their child's achievements! We make jokes all the time about kids who grow to be so much taller than both their parents, like asking to see a picture of the gardener or the guy who delivered the spring water! To answer the question, if a baby is a bit on the small side but is developing appropriately, eating well, and gaining weight every month, don't worry.

#128 *I really like to rock my son to sleep, but I've been warned against this. What do you think?*

I'm not against rocking, but when the baby gets used to rocking *all the time,* the minute you put him down on the bed, he'll wake up because the rocking has stopped. Babies love the rocking motion—in the car, in a swing, in mom's arms—but if you always rock him when you want him to take a nap or go to sleep for the night, that's what he'll get used to, and you won't be able to put him down until he's in a deep sleep—which can make bedtime a lot more unpleasant than it needs to be.

Years ago, I lost this argument with a young lady who told me, "This is my last baby, and I'm going to rock her to sleep." You know, the child never did get used to going to sleep alone in her bed. She's now nearly 10 and can fall asleep only on the couch or in her parents' bed. Pretty soon, she's going to get too big to carry back to bed. Then what? But her father's a cop, so I no longer argue the point!

I'm really torn. My doctor is usually great at giving me advice, but sometimes I just don't agree with him. He's been doing this for 25 years, and I've been a parent for about 20 minutes!

While many doctors—those you see on television and the ones in "real life"—espouse one particular method of raising children, I'm a firm believer that good parenting involves making good choices. Like in a Chinese restaurant, you can listen to all sides and then pick one from column A and two from column B, whatever works for you. On many issues, especially behavioral ones, if what you're doing *works for you,* it's okay, even if your doctor has a different point of view. People need to understand that there is more than one way to do this parenting thing. If there was only one way to do it, we'd write up a set of rules, maybe get an 800 number, and all the kids in the world would be the same.

#130

My baby wants to breast-feed almost continually—seems like every hour or so.

That's called grazing. Babies who graze learn to eat when they're upset and use food as a stress reliever. The problem with allowing this to continue is that this habit can follow them into adolescence and adulthood and become a chronic weight problem or even an eating disorder. Feed the baby only at proper intervals, certainly not less than every three hours, under normal circumstances.

In between feedings, you may give the baby water, sugar water (one teaspoon of sugar to four ounces of water) or diluted chamomile tea.

#131 *The baby seems to have teeny, tiny white-heads on her nose and cheeks. A little early for teenage breakout?*

This isn't teenage breakout—or even baby acne. It is probably a condition called milia, caused by underdeveloped sweat glands. This condition is not at all serious and corrects itself as the sweat glands develop, usually by the time the baby is about three months old. Just leave the spots alone. No pressure, no squeezing, no lotions. Just time.

#132 *I heard that last year was a doozie for ear infections. Is there anything I can do to avoid the problem this year?*

Unfortunately, no. There's not a whole lot you can do to prevent ear infections, but there are a few tricks of the trade for dealing with recurring infections. If the baby has several ear infections, you'll want to ask your doctor about checking for allergies. Or it may just be an older sibling bringing colds home from school. You might ask about putting the baby on prophylactic antibiotics as a preventative measure, or consider putting ventilation tubes in the ears when he gets a little older (a minor surgical procedure, but one that parents swear by when they see their child stop the continual suffering).

Day-care kids often pass around winter colds for what seems like months because of their close quarters and predilection for putting everything in the mouth. It's just one of those things we look at as a trade-off in an otherwise good situation.

Should I keep a hat on him in the cold weather?

If you're east of the Rockies, sure. A hat helps to keep body heat constant. It won't prevent the baby from picking up viruses that he may come in contact with, but it will make him more comfortable in the cold, cold weather. Besides, those ear flaps are cute. But for those of you who live in more moderate climates where a cold winter's day is 60 degrees, please don't overdress your baby. Lightweight hats are fine, but save those furry hats and mufflers for trips to the snow.

#134 *My friend's baby just had a febrile seizure, and it was petrifying. How serious are they?*

A febrile seizure, which may occur between the ages of three months and five years, is a short convulsion associated with a high fever. It usually lasts 20 to 40 seconds, during which the baby's eyes roll back in his head, his arms twitch, and he may even lose consciousness briefly. It *is* very frightening. If the seizure lasts 30 seconds, to any normal parent it feels like 30 minutes. But it is not serious; it is *not* epilepsy/convulsive disorder, and it absolutely does not cause brain damage.

However, although the seizure itself is neither uncommon nor dangerous, an infant should be seen by a physician after one occurs, in order to check for any underlying infection that should be treated (the most common are ear infections, tonsillitis, bladder infections, and roseola). It is also important to exclude a disease of the central nervous system, such as meningitis.

#135 *What do I do if it happens to my baby?*

When a baby has a febrile convulsion, the first thing you want to do is get her temperature down right away. Soak some towels in *tepid* (not cold) water and wrap her in them. Or put her into a tepid bath. Use a fever-reducing suppository (which you should always have on hand in the fridge).

Most of the time, by the time the rescue squad comes (if you called 911), or by the time you get to the doctor's office, the baby is either smiling or asleep.

A controversy currently exists over appropriate post-seizure treatment. Some doctors recommend that about 15 days after the seizure, the child should undergo an electroencephalogram to see if the brain waves are normal. And some still favor the use of anticonvulsants (phenobarbital) for two or three years, but we don't do that anymore in our office.

These seizures happen to a lot of kids. *A lot* of kids.

Can I prevent a fever seizure?

To a certain extent, yes. If there's a family history of febrile—or fever—seizures, which may make the baby more susceptible, and he runs a high fever, keep him in light clothing and in a cool room. Don't put him in sleepers with feet, because it's like basting a turkey. If a tiny baby has a 101-degree fever, and you put him in a sleeper in the afternoon and it gets very warm, you'll just roast him and his temperature could shoot to 106. If your baby has indeed had a fever seizure—which means he *may* be more susceptible to having another—you want to follow the tips above, plus treat with ibuprofen for fevers above 100 degrees instead of the recommended 102. If your child has never had a seizure and there is no family history, there's really nothing you can do to prevent one, except to keep an infant or child with a fever in an environment that's cool.

#137 *How do I go about clipping those tiny nails?*

I suggest not clipping nails because they're so tiny the baby will probably be a year old before you finish the first hand. So, don't clip, buff. Go to a beauty supply store and buy the kind of soft, white nail buffer that manicurists use. You'll both be a lot happier.

#138 *I've heard horror stories about DPT shots and other immunizations. Does the baby really need to have them?*

Absolutely. Not giving a baby a shot against pertussis (whooping cough) is a form of abuse. It really is. When you look at the statistics regarding the untoward reactions to these diphtheria/pertussis/tetanus shots, it is really infinitesimal, but it has been overplayed by the news media and the talk shows. These are preventable diseases, and it is a crime not to inoculate your child against them. Even the new chickenpox vaccine is doing well. The kids who do get reactions to the shot usually get four or five pox that last only 24 hours.

#139 *Two grandmas, two opinions. So tell me, do I wake my infant up to eat—or not???*

Well, yes and no. You do want to create a schedule for the baby, and you don't want him to go longer than four hours without eating. So *that's* when you wake him. At night, however, after that last feeding at 11 o'clock or so, he can sleep as long as he wants, as long as you start the next day at more or less the same time. So go tell each of the grandmas that she was right!

#140 *I should wake my child up just to get her on a schedule? In other words, am I crazy???*

Yes, you should wake her—no, you're not crazy. Even if you look at every nap as a gift, wake the baby in order to make a schedule. You will be much happier knowing when she is going to get up rather than playing "catch-as-catch-can." You may think the nap you're interrupting is a necessity for the kid, but it is *absolutely* a necessity for the mom. Better to get the baby on a schedule early so that you *know* when you'll be able to get some rest!

#141 *I know a new mom who called her pediatrician so often he finally told her to find another doctor. How much is too much?*

People who make an unreasonable amount of phone calls do so because they are so unsure of themselves and/or are listening to other people too much. I can tell now after 32 years when somebody has put something into a new mother's ear.

I remember years ago, our office had something called the Yearly Plan. It used to be somewhere between $65 and $120 dollars a year for as many visits as you wanted to make during the year—there was no extra charge (that tells you just how many years ago it must have been). I know a woman who absolutely broke the world's record—100 visits in a year. There were times she came in twice in one day! She didn't call, she just showed up. If we didn't have the Yearly Plan, she most certainly would have called.

I don't think mothers who have first babies are supposed to be sure of themselves. And I think it's okay to call the doctor, but I think quite often *when you have five questions in the morning, four of them will be answered by your own good common sense by the afternoon.* But as pediatricians, part of our responsibility is to answer questions by phone. It goes with the territory.

Call the doctor when you need to. Don't hesitate. Just use common sense. If you have a few questions (and you're not dealing with an emergency), make a list and call toward the end of the day. The doctor will certainly appreciate your consideration and respond in kind.

#142 *I've been breast-feeding for only a month or so. Is this long enough?*

Yes. Breast-feeding is your choice and when to stop is your choice also. If a month is long enough for you, it's long enough for me.

#143 *Do babies run fevers from teething?*

No. This is what is known in the medical profession as a *bubbe meisa* (translation: grandma's story or old wives' tale) first told to me by my own bubbe.

Never associate fever with teething. If your infant has a fever of over 100.5 and is at the age where teething is active—beginning at three to four months until about two years of age—do not brush it off as "just teething." There could be an infection that goes unwatched, unheeded and, if left untreated, can lead to a serious problem.

Do babies get diarrhea when they're teething?

I'd like to say a resounding *no* to this one, too, but I sometimes get a lot of heat when I do. I've got one mother who swears that her baby never had any crankiness or crying usually associated with cutting a tooth. But when he would get the runs for no apparent reason, she would put her finger in his mouth and find that a tiny new tooth had broken through.

One explanation may be that babies generally drink more fluids when they're cutting a tooth than when they're not, and that may account for the diarrhea. But the truth is, at the age when babies are teething, they put everything from the floor into their mouths—including dirt—and that could cause diarrhea. When a baby has diarrhea, it's generally because of something he ate that disagreed with him, or a flu. Blaming it on teething is a great excuse.

So although some moms and even some colleagues disagree, I think the association between diarrhea and teething should be filed along with the above question under "b" for baloney.

#145 *I've heard bourbon is good when the baby is teething.*

Bourbon is good for the *parent* when the baby is teething. For the baby, there are many treatments for teething. Some are combinations that physicians have made up, others are natural remedies found at health food stores. I often recommend an oral dose of Tylenol or children's Motrin. Motrin (or Advil) is ibuprofen, an anti-inflammatory which is excellent for teething in a young infant.

Will the baby sleep through the night in my lifetime?

It's true, one of the greatest days in the lives of new parents begins on the morning after the new baby has slept through the night for the first time. If your baby is healthy, this can happen anywhere from two to five months or so. It is a little more difficult for breast-feeding mothers to discontinue the night feeding as early as those who bottle-feed. First, because even if the baby's not hungry, you're going to have to empty that breast. And second, because babies are more reluctant to give up the breast-feeding experience than a bottle.

So for whenever you and baby are ready, here is Dr. Zukow's Patented, Foolproof, 100% Guaranteed Procedure for Getting Your Baby to Sleep Through the Night. First, let's define "night" as 11 P.M. to 6 A.M. You want to get the baby's last feeding in as close to 11 P.M. as possible, which is not an indecent hour, especially if she sleeps until 6 A.M. at two, three, four, or even five months.

For the first three nights, when she wakes up at 3 A.M. (or whatever time she is accustomed to waking up), you give her a bottle of diluted formula (half formula, half water). On the fourth, fifth, and sixth night, she still gets a bottle, but only of water. On the seventh, eighth, and ninth night, when she awakens, you walk in, pat her on the back and walk out of the room. After only nine days, presto! That's it! Usually.

Okay, you may hear some crying when she gets nothing to drink at all. But there's never been any evidence that you shouldn't allow a baby to cry. I don't believe letting a baby cry is abusive, nor do I believe that you're not bonding. Crying is her way of expressing herself and getting your attention. I don't believe she can do any real harm to herself by crying. And, if you as parents can live through a few tough nights of crying while giving up the night feeding, you will be rewarded by peaceful nights from now on—until she starts dating.

#147

If the baby is flushed, should I take his temperature?

You can if you wish, but I would undress the baby first to see if he isn't just overdressed.

#148

I always heard from my older sister how important it is to cover the baby's ears in cold weather. Is this so?

When cold air hits the eardrum, it can cause pain. So if you live near Lake Michigan, go ahead and pull the flaps down. For our readers in warmer climates, it's generally not necessary.

#149

When my baby was getting a blood test, the technician said, "Don't worry, the baby doesn't feel any pain." He sure cried loud for a kid who didn't feel anything. What do you think?

I think that anyone who tells you babies don't feel pain is living in the Dark Ages. They used to do surgery on babies with very little anesthetic, but someone finally realized that they *must* feel pain. Now they give babies morphine. If you don't believe that getting a baby's heel stuck two or three times hurts a little, stick your own heel two or three times.

How long should I breast-feed?

Some say three months, others six, others much longer. Working moms who go back to work in about three months tell me that that time frame is pretty satisfactory. While most moms will stop at three, four, or six months, there are those who will go on past a year. When you stop is a personal choice, but I am a firm believer that a child shouldn't ask for a breast and the car keys in the same conversation.

I feel so tied down since I'm the only one who feeds this kid. It's like I'm the local gas station. Fill 'er up!

It does tie you down, and it is also much harder to get the baby on a schedule if you're breast-feeding since you can't tell how much he is getting. (If you ask me, the breast should have little circles around it indicating one ounce, two ounces, and so on. But nobody ever asked me.) Many moms pump breast milk or supplement feedings with a formula bottle so that the baby can be fed by someone other than herself. Doing a little shopping or getting out for an occasional dinner or a movie can be a very liberating experience when you're a nursing mother.

#152 *I've heard that a new baby has a "natural immunity." Exactly what does that mean?*

Because of the blood passed from mother to child, a new baby *is,* indeed, born with what is commonly referred to as a "natural immunity," that is, the innate ability to fight common infections until his own immune system matures and takes over at somewhere between six months and a year old. However, during these first few months, the baby can be extremely susceptible to specific serious viruses and bacteria not fought by the shared-blood immunity his mom gave him. That is a primary reason the baby needs to be monitored closely by the pediatrician during the first 12 to 18 months of life.

#153

What about milk allergies?

One of the most common allergies a baby has is to cow's milk. When we even suspect a milk allergy, we'll often take the breast-feeding mother off of cow's milk, cheese, and other dairy products and the baby does fine. Or if a baby has a problem with one of the common formulas like Similac or Enfamil, we'll switch him to a soy formula and see how he does. Surprisingly often, avoiding milk products cures a variety of symptoms, including colic, rashes, abnormal bowel movements, and excess spitting.

That doesn't mean babies are going to have this sensitivity forever, but with so many products now on the market that are lactose-free or promote lactose tolerance, there are a lot of ways to go these days without compromising nutrition for the baby.

#154

How important are vitamins?

I generally start vitamins with fluoride at two to three months of age. It depends on where in the country you live and the fluoride content of your local water. Babies don't always drink enough water on a regular basis to get the benefit of fluoride—that's why we give it as a supplement. We see fewer cavities when the teeth come in because of it.

#155 *What makes the baby spit up so much?*

They drink too much, too fast. Some babies are just fast swallowers, and they wind up swallowing a lot of air. If spitting up is not associated with weight loss or poor weight gain, it is not significant except that you'll have to buy yourself a plastic shawl. Nine times out of ten, if you're dressed up to go out and pick up the baby to say good night, the baby will spit up. A law of nature, I guess.

#156 *Is it at all preventable or should I just get used to yucky shoulders on all of my clothing?*

For a baby who spits up a lot, occasionally formula changes will help. Try going from cow's milk formula to a soy formula or even a meat-based formula. Changing the baby's position during and after feedings may be a solution. Keeping the baby in a semi-sitting position after a meal should reduce some spitting up.

#157 *Do those baby bottles with plastic inserts and "nursing" nipples help spitters?*

No, not really. Some moms do like them, obviously, or they wouldn't be on the market, but I find they really don't help spitters. Spitters, if they don't have a physical problem causing the spitting, generally are being overfed or are eating too fast. Modify one or the other, or both, and you will no doubt get less spitting.

#158 *In fact, does it really matter what kind of baby bottle I use?*

No. Since you're the one feeding the baby most often, use what is comfortable for you. They have baby bottles in so many new shapes and sizes these days, they don't even look like baby bottles. As long as they have the means to get the milk or juice from the bottle into the kid, it's okay.

#159 *Just how early do you think you can discipline a new baby?*

I once heard that the earliest you can discipline an infant is in utero. Legend has it that a pregnant mother heard her unborn baby "crying" and gave her stomach a real hard slap and the baby stopped. With the advent of fathers and mothers talking, singing, and playing music to their unborn infants, the first thing I would recommend is to tell the baby to sleep through the night, eat every four hours, and sleep late on Sundays.

My belief is that discipline is just another word for control. This starts with your own self-discipline, which begins as early as when you come home from the hospital with that infant. Getting the baby on a schedule that allows you to have some time for yourself is the first evidence of "discipline" for a baby. However, during the first year, discipline only really comes into play with regard to the baby's safety, like smacking the hand of a six-month-old who touches the light socket or scolding an early walker who continually heads for the street. You'll find that it's more effective to remove the baby from unsafe situations than to try to convince her to modify her behavior. There'll be plenty of time for discipline in the second year and beyond, so don't worry too much about it during the first year. Just enjoy the baby!

#160 *What should I expect from my parents and in-laws as grandparents?*

There are still some bubbes and papas around. Characteristically, these are grandparents who genuinely want to devote whatever spare time they have to being grandparents. It may be just because they really do love the grandchildren or, perhaps, because they see a rebirth, another chance at raising children. They're wiser at this point in their lives because they learned from their own mistakes in raising their own children, or maybe they feel they didn't make any mistakes and raised the "perfect" child. But for the most part, contemporary grandparents are hardworking, trip-taking, life-living people. They love the grandchildren but have a life of their own and appreciate the fact that it's okay to allow their children to raise their own children.

#161 *Why are grandparents often overprotective?*

I think the main reason grandparents are overprotective is that they don't have a lot of faith in you as a child-rearer—that's what I have found in private practice. Why do they give so much advice? Because they're living their lives over again through their sons or daughters via their grandchildren.

#162 *If I bottle-feed from the beginning, how much formula do I give?*

You might have a baby who takes two ounces every three hours or one who will chug-a-lug four to six ounces by the time he's a week old. It depends on the baby. The bottom line is that it's not how much you give the baby, but what makes him happy and helps to make a good schedule.

Remember two things here: the rule of thumb—you don't want to give him more than 32 ounces of liquid a day—and keeping the baby happy does *not* mean falling into the trap of demand feeding.

#163 *How do I know how and when to increase the amount?*

If the baby is on a good four-hour schedule and is taking, for example, 3 ounces every four hours, or 18 ounces per day, and all of a sudden the baby demands food in three hours, you know he's hungry and you have to increase the amount. Start increasing each feeding by half an ounce and see how the baby does. If he's finishing the bottle and goes back to the four-hour schedule, fine. If you still hear from him in three hours, you can increase by another half ounce per feeding, up to a total of 32 ounces per day.

When should I start the baby on solid food?

It's really the baby who calls the shots on this one, but you need to remember two very important things: (1) it's not healthy for her to have more than 32 ounces of liquid a day, and (2) it's not necessary for her to be breast-fed every single hour on demand. If you're finding she is less and less satisfied with each feeding, you can consider cereal as early as four weeks. If she is used to being fed every four hours and suddenly sends you a message three hours after feedings, then it's time to start solid food.

#165 *Does giving the baby cereal that early help get him on a schedule?*

Yes. You can give a baby solid food to help get him on a schedule, and *you* will know to start when you find he's just not satisfied with the bottle or breast. Also, you'll avoid causing a "good eater" from filling up on just fluids because cereal takes up more room in the stomach than milk.

You will read here in several answers that the baby should not consume more than 32 ounces of liquid a day. Some babies will drink up to a gallon a day if they were allowed to, because it's a lot easier to do than chewing up food.

When during the meal do I feed the cereal to the baby—at the beginning, the middle, or the end?

My recommendation is to feed babies the bottle, then solid food, then bottle. They're usually so hungry at the beginning of the meal, they'll most often grab the spoon if you try to give them cereal first. If you abate a little of that hunger with part of a bottle, they'll cooperate much more readily when cereal time comes.

#167 *When I tried to give the baby cereal, she gave it back to me (and the wallpaper) in a giant raspberry. What am I doing wrong?*

Nothing. Although you may think the raspberry is an editorial comment on your food preparation, it's probably the consistency of the cereal she's unaccustomed to. Plus the raspberry is a great noise and will be repeated when we laugh often enough. Try the following:

Day 1: Add just one teaspoon of baby rice cereal to an ounce of formula (or pumped breast milk) in a small bowl. It will be pretty soupy, but she'll start to get the taste of the cereal. Let her finish the bottle or nurse as usual afterward.

Day 2: Increase the amount of cereal to two teaspoons to an ounce of formula. This will change the consistency slightly. She'll probably drink less milk in the following feeding.

Day 3: Increase to three teaspoons of cereal to an ounce of formula (if it's too sticky, increase formula to attain desired consistency).

#168 *This baby has become the cereal monster, wanting more and more with every meal. How much can I give her?*

You can keep increasing the cereal until you reach 3 to 3 1/2 tablespoons *dry* per meal. It will, of course, take most of the bottle to get to the appropriate consistency, but she'll be much more satisfied than with less cereal and more formula.

Won't I create a fat baby if I start solid food before six months?

About 15 years ago, the American Academy of Pediatrics said that pediatricians are creating obese children by giving solid food too early. I refuse to accept that notion. If you give your child a gallon of milk and a pound of cereal every day, yes, you will have an obese child. But if you follow your pediatrician's recommendations about quantities of food, and you see an appropriate weight gain each month (one to two pounds under usual circumstances), you can avoid obesity.

It is generally recommended that a baby's weight at five months should be about double his birth weight. At a year, his weight should be about triple his birth weight (this is just for the average weight—it is not necessary for a baby who was 10 pounds at birth to weigh 30 pounds at a year).

Please understand that these are only recommendations and are not written in stone and should not be treated as if they were.

#170 *How do I add foods to the baby's diet?*

That's easy. Pick just one new food and add it to the diet over three or four days. Add one cereal, then one fruit, one vegetable, one "meat" (lamb, turkey, or chicken) at a time. Make sure you do wait several days before introducing a new food. If you add new foods too quickly, and the baby develops an allergic reaction, the kid'll be in college before you find out what the culprit food is. *Warning:* DO NOT sweeten any food with honey to make it more palatable. Honey should not be fed to infants under one year of age as it may be a source of the botulism organism.

#171 *If the baby is allergic to a food, what kind of symptoms would I see?*

Most often, whatever food is the culprit will cause the baby to develop a rash. There are some babies, however, in whom allergies manifest themselves in the form of wheezing, congested nose, or diarrhea. And some babies who are sensitive to cow's milk may even get constipated. Different foods can cause different reactions, but the reaction I see most often is a rash.

How fat is too fat?

In 33 years of practice, I've never heard a parent say, "Isn't he just right?" According to parents and grandparents, all babies are either too thin or too fat. The American Academy of Pediatrics issues a series of national averages of height and weight for children, but I don't believe in looking at them very often—only when clinically indicated. It's that harping on the baby being too thin or too fat that can lead to eating problems later on.

What is too fat? Probably a baby who gains more than 2 to 2 1/2 pounds per month. This may lead to obesity in later life. Fat babies—really fat babies—may grow into fat adults as a result of a combination of eating habits and genetics. There's not much you can do about genes, but you *can* control what goes into that baby's mouth.

#173 *How can I get the baby not to overeat without feeling like I'm depriving him?*

What can you do? You can wean him down *slowly* off of eating too much. You can't put babies on a diet, like adults, but you can wean them down so that each day or two you're decreasing *slightly* the quantity of food. Then they get into the habit of eating smaller portions and being satisfied. The habit of eating all the time is broken, and *you* break *your* habit of feeding in order to encourage a particular behavior. This is especially important for parents who find out that if you feed him, he's quiet, he's nice, he smiles. And look how nice and big he's getting.

Remember that at one time in history, being fat meant being successful. If you were rotund, you were the owner. If you were thin, you were the worker. Our own parents thought that fat was wonderful. If you couldn't pinch a cheek, the baby was malnourished. It's only in the last 20 years or so that we've changed our thinking about fat babies; we've wised up.

#174 *My newborn sneezes a lot, but I can't believe she already has a cold!*

Although it is possible for a newborn to catch a little cold, newborns are also known to sneeze when they are in bright light, like bright sunshine. Being exposed to dust or the dander from animals is another reason she may sneeze a lot. This sneezing is nothing to worry about and actually helps clear out her nasal passages. *Gesundheit!*

If breast-feeding hurts, should I give it up?

Again, *if* you breast-feed, *how long* you breast-feed, are your own choices. If you are experiencing pain associated with breast-feeding, the pain may not be a permanent condition. It could come and go. It may get easier for you, or it may cause you more discomfort than you think it is worth. No one can make the decision to quit for you. Just be assured that you are no less a "good mom" if you need to switch to the bottle.

#176

My whole family eats a low-fat diet. Is this harmful to the baby as she starts to eat what we eat?

I am a proponent of a low-fat diet. For adults. A baby doesn't need to be on a low-fat diet and shouldn't be. If you're worried that your baby's overweight, decrease the amount of food she eats and the number of feedings, not the fat.

So is formula better than milk, because it has more fat?

Babies do need fat. That is a fact. One of the reasons that the formula manufacturers have succeeded in promoting the recommendation that babies stay on formula for so long is because it provides the necessary fat for kids who are not yet taking solid food. Once a baby eats solid food, however, a well-balanced diet will provide both the necessary fat and calories. So if the baby is thriving, you're not starving that baby's nervous system of the fat it needs. I have very healthy Rhodes scholars who were on low-fat milk and solid food when they were two months old.

#178 *You must get a lot of questions on how to feed the baby. Any favorites?*

Oh, yes. A father called me at about three o'clock in the afternoon and said, "I'm really in trouble. Remember you started Andy on solid food?" I said I did. "Well, I gave him a teaspoon of the cereal and now the spoon is stuck in his mouth." I then recalled that Andy is only two months old.

"So, pull it out!" I told the father.

"Every time I try to pull the spoon out, he sucks it right back into his mouth," he said.

I asked, "How long have you been trying to feed him like this?"

He said, "About 45 minutes."

I almost fell off the chair. I was laughing so hard I had to call the man back.

"Is this stupid, or what?"

"No, the baby created a vacuum and you were afraid to break it." I felt so bad for this guy, but the story makes me laugh to this day.

#179 *I didn't have my son circumcised at birth. Can I still change my mind?*

Yes, but remember, the longer you wait, the more pain is involved—so if you change your mind about circumcision, discuss it with your doctor immediately.

I really want this middle of the night stuff to be over as quickly as possible. Anything else I should remember?

Yes. If you have a healthy baby who continues to wake up in the middle of the night, here's a short but effective list of *DON'TS:*

1. Don't allow him to sleep with you.
2. Don't feed him.
3. Don't rock him.
4. Don't walk him.
5. Don't sing to him.
6. Don't even whistle.

#181 *So many of the parenting techniques that I favor differ so greatly with the way my parents did it!*

What is applicable in our society today may not be applicable at all 10 years from now or 20 years from now—just as what is applicable today is different from 10 or 20 years ago. The technological advances that have been made and the advances in health care all have a tremendous influence on what is going to happen in the future. So take what you like from your parents' techniques, and leave the rest. Believe me, your kids will say the same thing about the way you did it!

Should I keep track of what percentile my child is in?

The fact that you're asking the question illustrates why percentiles are not a good idea. In fact, I have a very personal vendetta against them. They do very little other than cause anxiety among parents who inevitably compare their child's percentiles with those of their friends' children. As the child grows, that anxiety can be transferred to the child, especially if she becomes aware of constantly being compared to others. If your baby is healthy and showing appropriate weight gain, leave the percentiles alone. You don't need them.

#183 *If he swallows something he shouldn't, should I make him vomit?*

In most cases, the child has to be made to vomit if he has taken a poison. As soon as your baby becomes at all mobile, you should have a bottle of ipecac syrup on hand to induce vomiting. *Warning:* The exception is gasoline or a kerosene product, because it is more dangerous for a baby to inhale this sort of product than for it to go through the gastrointestinal tract. So don't make him vomit for that.

But I don't keep any poison in the house.

You might not realize it, but many of the substances you have in the house could be toxic to babies, including many cleaning products and, of course, medications. Some very beautiful plants that you may have in the house or in the yard can be poisonous if ingested. Keep all cleaning products and medications out of the baby's reach, and get rid of any toxic plants or bushes in the house or yard. Your local poison control center can help you identify the toxic plants and substances. Remember, *don't underestimate a baby who is mobile.* They disappear as quick as lightning and get into things that could be very dangerous. This happens to even the "best" of parents, so please don't take these warnings lightly.

Who should I call if the baby swallows something poisonous?

Don't waste time trying to reach the doctor. Get the number of a local poison control center and keep it by the phone with your other emergency numbers. If she has eaten or drunk something poisonous, you don't want to be looking for the Yellow Pages.

#186

The baby just swallowed my last birth control pill. Should I worry?

Not about the baby.

#187 *My baby threw up, and I'd swear it hit someone in the next room! Is this normal?*

This is called projectile vomiting, and it's true, it can shoot across the room. If it happens once or twice, it may just be because someone has moved the baby too quickly. However, if it persists with your new baby (three to six weeks old) and/or there are dry diapers and an absence of stool, the doctor should be consulted immediately to check for an intestinal obstruction. If the baby is older, it could be the flu, or spoiled food, and you should just be alert to the possibility of dehydration.

If the baby is just doing a great deal of excess spitting, however, he may have a condition called reflux, which means that spasms occur where the esophagus meets the stomach and the food is shot back up. Fortunately, there is medication that works very well to treat reflux.

#188 *Now that my baby is moving around more, I notice that he keeps bumping his head—and hard! How can I make sure he's not severely injured?*

Infants who just begin to walk or even crawl are wobbly. And the shortest distance between two points is a straight line, even if there happens to be a table or the fire pit in the way. Over the years, I've found that Styrofoam bumpers on coffee tables will avoid a lot of injuries. Coffee table corners are magnets for kids' heads.

When the baby gets a bump on the forehead or on the back of the head (and that's a "when" not an "if") you may see a hematoma, a collection of blood under the skin caused by the breaking of a superficial blood vessel, causing a bump, sometimes as big as a golf ball. If the child cries right away and there's no vomiting, if you look at his eyes and the pupils are equal, you probably don't have a problem at that time. Most of the time, the remedy is a kiss on the boo-boo.

However, if you are unsure *at all,* phone the pediatrician. She will help you evaluate the degree of trauma. You'll be asked about the crying, vomiting, and pupils. Also, was he knocked unconscious? Was there bleeding or fluid coming out of the ear? You should be asked to feel the soft spot and make sure it's soft and flat, not bulging. This information will help the doctor determine whether or not the baby needs to be seen right away, if at all.

#189 *I've been reading the child development books, and my child isn't doing what they say she should be doing. Should I be concerned?*

You've got to remember one important fact: Your baby hasn't read the books. Every child develops at a different rate. You have to take into consideration the whole child, not just the fact that the child may not be crawling at six months. Is she alert? Does she respond to your voice? Is she rolling over? Well, if she's doing all these things but doesn't crawl like the neighbor's baby does, it just doesn't make any difference. If she doesn't walk at a year, but says, "Hello, Mama," I'd be surprised if there was anything wrong with her.

Of course, your doctor is trained to keep an eye on her development. Don't be shy about voicing your concern to your doctor. That's part of establishing a productive, long-term relationship with the medical professional who may well be a part of your child's life—and, by extension, yours—for a very long time.

#190 *My seven-month-old seems mesmerized by the television. I feel a little guilty, but it keeps her out of my hair. Is that okay?*

Face it. Television is a baby-sitter. It even baby-sits for me. My wife says, "Go watch the TV for a while." It's not all that bad to sit the kid in front of the TV, but you really do have to limit the time. It's perfectly okay in small doses, say if you want to do the dishes in peace, or you want to talk to a friend for 15 minutes. Just use common sense about the content. Babies love the color and motion of cartoons, and even very young ones can respond to the music and physical activity in shows like "Barney" and "Lambchop's Play-along." Of course, "Sesame Street" has a little something for everyone. I would avoid loud car chases, shootouts, and blood and guts.

#191 *I've heard some kids become biters as soon as they get teeth. How do I discourage this uncharming habit?*

The most dangerous bite known to mankind is the human bite. I personally have seen the tip of a mother's nose having been bitten off by an 11-month-old. I've seen a sibling's earlobe bitten off. Nothing is more dangerous. The treatment for this is very aggressive. It doesn't do any good to hit or to bite the kid back. The best thing to do is put a slice of soap in his mouth. It has to be done each and every time he bites. You might not see this very often in the first year of life, but if the baby is a biter, better watch out when he gets a full set of teeth.

#192 *My daughter just isn't an eater, but I'm afraid to push food on her. I'd hate to be the cause of a weight problem later in life.*

Maybe the most important part of that question is when you say, "I'd hate to be the cause of a weight problem." That's something that we're much more aware of these days, much more than your mother was. And, because we are so aware of it, we're better equipped to avoid the common pitfall of overstuffing our kids. Mothers who are afraid to push food on kids are smart. The best thing to do is to put a small amount of food in front of the baby, and if she finishes it, great, give her a little more. And if she doesn't, wait until the next meal. She won't starve because she doesn't finish a meal (unless she's ill—and then you do have to watch her intake carefully, especially of liquids). Remember, as these kids enter the second year—maybe it starts at 10 months, maybe at 14 months—their appetites drop precipitously because they become much more active and much less interested in sitting still. And that's great. I'd much rather have a kid running around the house than sitting around all day eating.

I don't want to get in the habit of spanking, but sometimes this baby is so exasperating! What should I do?

To spank or not to spank. I'm told this one is controversial, but not to me. Personally, I am not a big fan of spanking. I think hitting begets hitting, just like yelling begets yelling. Sure, I hit my kids—when they put their feet in the street or their fingers in the light sockets. I wanted to leave an indelible mark, which some of them remember to this day, because these situations were life-threatening. My problem with spanking—and that's an old-fashioned term for hitting—is that typically when you go to hit the child, you're angry. And when you're angry, you're likely to hit the child too hard. That's what worries me. If you hit a baby who's at the crawling stage and you take a swing and hit too hard, you run the risk of breaking that baby's back. Believe me, this has been seen over and over in emergency rooms. Please understand, I'm not against discipline and I'm in favor of control, but I feel there's a better way.

I try not to be a hitter, but that makes me a champion hollerer. Is that harmful to her?

There's nothing wrong with raising your voice, as long as you're not belittling your child or calling her names. In the first year, babies may not understand every word you say, but they understand much more than we give them credit for—and more than that, they understand tone of voice. It's the frustration/fatigue syndrome that leads to real hollering. I wish no one ever felt the need to holler or scream, but that's not very realistic. If you find yourself at the end of your rope and absolutely have to let off steam, you might try hollering in a closet, instead of at the infant. The best discipline for a baby is a real stern and consistent "no" at least three times, and if that fails, move the culprit to another room.

#195 *My friend didn't leave the baby for six months. Then, when they finally did go out, the baby cried for three solid hours. How can I avoid that scene?*

I swear to you, if you get yourselves *and* the baby used to a certain amount of natural separation, these scenes can be avoided. Leave the baby. Go out. (I thought you were going to tell me that when your friend finally went out for the evening, *she* cried for three hours! But that's a different story altogether.)

#196 *I think I have my house childproof. Can you give me some essentials, just to make sure?*

Here are ten quick tips:

1. Keep all medications, even over-the-counter medications, out of her reach.
2. Check house and yard for any poisonous plants or bushes.
3. Use baby gates at stairways or to prevent her from getting into dangerous areas (like where tools or electrical appliances are kept).
4. If you have a pool or spa, make sure there's a gate and that it is secured at all times.

5. Cover electric sockets with plastic covers (available at all hardware stores and in most baby departments).
6. Cover pointed corners of any tables within her reach, including dining room and coffee tables.
7. Keep all breakables (china and crystal, for example) out of reach.
8. Buy a padded bathtub spout cover. Babies are so slippery in the tub that even when being bathed by competent adults, they could be injured by hitting their heads on the spout.
9. Install latches for cabinets, drawers, and even the toilet lid. Once a baby is mobile, she is so *fast* that she's going to get away from even the most watchful parent momentarily.
10. Make sure the crib and playpen have slats no more than 2 $\frac{3}{8}$" apart so she can't fit her head or body through them and get stuck.

The best way to childproof is to be smart and anticipate. Anticipate what could cause harm even if the baby is only five months old and rolling, because in what seems like just one day, she'll go from rolling to crawling and getting into things. In fact, I always recommend that parents get down on all fours and crawl around the house. This way, you can see the house from the baby's vantage point and will find all sorts of things that need babyproofing.

#197 *How important is it to socialize a baby early? I'm not working outside the home, and I want to take care of her all the time, all by myself.*

Socializing the baby early accomplishes three things:

1. It makes the transition to day care or preschool much, much easier if she's used to being around other adults as well as kids.
2. It allows the parent to have some time to herself, which will make her a more happy and relaxed mother.
3. It fosters independence and confidence in the child, which can only serve her well as she grows.

I'm afraid that the parent who walls herself off with an infant is going to be a parent who is going to stay walled off as the child grows. These are the parents who later will be "held hostage" by their child—they will be what I call "consumed parents."

#198 *Held hostage? Isn't this a bit extreme?*

Yes, but so is the behavior of a consuming child, like the three-year-old who was waiting in the examining room with his mother. As I walked in, I heard the child command, "Mommy, sit down!" And, boy, that mother sat. This is a mother whose world, whose every move, every thought, revolves around a child who issues commands—which are granted without question. This mother is a *consumed* parent. Not good for the mom. Not good for the child.

How do I avoid falling into that "consumed" trap?

1. Establish time for yourselves immediately, parent to parent.
2. Allow some early separation from the baby.
3. Learn that you don't have to live for the infant from day one.
4. Understand that maintaining your identity as a human being is *not* being selfish, nor is it depriving your child of his needs.

What about the other extreme?

I call them *consuming* parents. In the name of love, these parents control every move of the child, every moment of his day, with expectations that are almost always impossible for the child to attain.

What's the answer? A happy medium. A parent who is neither controlled by a child (yes, even a tiny baby) nor orchestrates the child's every move. The middle ground, allowing a parent to be a person while allowing a kid to be a kid in all the various stages of development—this is the ideal.

Parents who *strive* for the ideal, and *realize that perfection in parenting simply does not exist,* will raise happier, more well-adjusted children.

I want to start the baby at day care, but I've heard it's a germ factory. What can I do?

Everybody has germs. Germs are in the air. Unless you've totally isolated the infant, yourself, and any siblings, you're going to have a baby for whom at least one cold during the first year is common. If you keep the baby out of day care, he will develop something when he goes to nursery school.

If you keep him out of nursery school, he will be subjected to a germ-filled world of reality in kindergarten. I think the socialization of the child, unless the child is sickly or has a chronic illness, is as important as is good health. When we look at the whole picture and the development of this infant to toddler to child to adolescent to adult, it's the socialization that's going to get him the job, not whether he's had a lot of colds.

My six-month-old crawls and says da-da and ma-ma. Does this mean he's supersmart? How do I know if I should enroll him in a special class?

Enjoy his infancy—it goes so fast, it'll be over before you know it. If he is supersmart, he always will be. Infancy and toddler stages are golden, untouched by societal pressures. Just let him be a baby and have fun watching him develop at his own pace. Special classes can come later, but babyhood is a fleeting moment. On the other hand, if he crawls over to the piano, pulls himself to a standing position and plays Mozart flawlessly, it's entirely another story.

#203 *Why are some babies so easy to deal with? My child is so difficult to feed, difficult to get to sleep, just plain difficult.*

When you're dealing with an infant, you have to consider the basic personality of the child, as well as your own. A relaxed parent will naturally find her baby easier to deal with. Some parents are born more confident; nothing bothers them, including the infant crying or whether he eats a lot or sleeps a lot or anything else. But most parents are so busy trying to be "perfect" at the beginning that it makes them not cool, not relaxed. That's why first babies are generally more difficult to deal with than second and third babies.

And then there are babies who just have tough personalities. I have probably had about a dozen babies throughout my years in practice who were tough. Temper tantrums from the very beginning, no matter what we tried. We thought it was colic, we thought it was a hernia, we thought it was a hundred different things. Then, all of a sudden at eight or nine months, they became pleasant babies. You can't call it, you can't change it. You just have to weather the storm. It will pass.

#204 *The baby has had several colds and is only eight months old. What am I doing wrong?*

As I said before, a cold or two before the end of the first year is not uncommon, especially if there's an older sibling or you belong to a "Mommy & Me" group, or the baby is in day care. Colds are airborne. If both parents are working parents, I think the chances of the infant getting frequent colds are increased.

What can I do?

Check out the baby for allergies. It may be dietary—if you're breast-feeding and the baby has these symptoms, it may be an allergy to milk and dairy products that's being transferred to the baby. You really can't isolate yourself or your baby from catching a cold. But you can wash your hands frequently throughout the day with an antibacterial soap, especially after diaper changes. Civilizations have survived millions of colds for millions of years, and your baby will, too.

#206 *Two of my friends' kids have been diagnosed ADHD. Is there any such thing as detection during the first year?*

This is a very important question, but attention deficit–hyperactivity disorder (ADHD) is very, very difficult to diagnose during the first year. Behavior that might signal ADHD in a five-year-old is normal for a baby. A baby's attention span, at 10 months, for example, is not very long, and the frustration level is naturally greater in a young infant or toddler, than in an older child. So the disorder is very tough, at best, to identify.

#207 *Parenthood takes so much energy, is it truly for the young, or is the maturity of a parent directly related to the ability to rear a child?*

There's no question that adjusting to parenthood takes energy. It is acknowledged that parenthood is the hardest job there is, young or not so young. Today's working parents tend to have their children when they're older—often thirtyish and above—and I think, in fact, maturation helps.

I grant you, it would be great for all parents to have the energy of a 22-year-old. However, the advantage of being over 30 or even 40 is that your life may be better organized with different priorities. Financially, you're probably more secure, so that's one less worry as the child's growing up. A great example are the fathers who are involved with second families, at which time they've already paid down the mortgage on the house and are earning a better living than they were 20 years ago. Now they have the time to take the kids to the baseball game, time to go on a picnic with them. It appears to be less pressure on them.

#208 *The baby swallowed a penny! What shall I do?*

If there is no choking, you don't have to do anything. Anything and everything that is movable and can fit into those chubby little hands will eventually reach the mouth. The penny will "come out in the wash." However, if he should swallow a quarter, *now* you're talking about serious money! (Sorry, old joke.)

#209 *I'm sure I would panic if I saw the baby was choking. Help me to be prepared.*

First of all, one amazing quality of parenthood is that it creates superhumans out of ordinary people. Even if you think you would panic, when it's *your* child in trouble, you will remain more calm than you thought possible. For an infant, the easiest thing to do is to put the baby facedown on your lap and stick your finger down the back of his throat. He'll vomit and he'll be fine. If he still has something lodged in his throat, try to take it out with your finger. *If he's having trouble breathing, call 911 immediately—don't waste time trying to reach your pediatrician.*

#210 *My baby puts everything under the sun into her mouth. I don't want to seem like a germ freak, but shouldn't I be worried?*

No. Even if she eats the dog food or cigarette butts, it all "comes out in the wash." What you do have to worry about are plants that are poisonous, medications you have in the house, and any kind of gasoline product. Poison centers generally recommend *not* making the baby vomit if she gets into gasoline or kerosene because it's better for her to get rid of it through the gastrointestinal tract than to bring it up and inhale it into the lungs.

All dangerous products and medications—including medications used for the baby—should be locked up. Remember, there is *no such thing* as a "childproof" top. *Don't* trust and *don't* underestimate any baby who is mobile.

My ten-month-old girl prefers playing with hammers and trucks to dolls and stuffed animals. Does this mean she has more of a chance of growing up gay?

No! The current school of thought is that sexual preference is decided by genetic makeup, not the trucks or the dolls.

Are early walkers and talkers the brightest children?

I don't believe that walking early and talking early are necessarily associated with being the brightest. I think the environment that is offered a developing infant is of greater importance. Maturation is an ongoing process—a process that lasts a lifetime, thank God.

#213

I've always been taught not to put anything smaller than an elbow into the ear. How do I clean those tiny little ears?

Gently. With a Q-tip after a bath. Don't dig around. Ask your pediatrician or the nurse in the pediatrician's office to show you how to twist a Q-tip in and twist it out without poking the eardrum. Sometimes it helps to have someone hold the baby's head. There might be times when the pediatrician will want to clean out some of the wax, because when we look at an ear, especially if the infant is fussy with a little bit of a cold, we want to make sure we can see what we're looking for, which is whether or not the baby has an ear infection.

How will I ever get a meal cooked with this baby underfoot?

Once a baby crawls and can move around and is at your feet all the time, you must arrange for her to have a place to play that is safe. (Many years ago I designed a room that had four cement walls, a cement floor, and three drains, plus a place to keep toys. At the end of the day, when the toys were picked up, you could just wash down the floor. No one bought it! Go figure.) She can't be crawling around in the kitchen when you're cooking. You've got to keep her entertained, but you may find she has too many toys. The trick is to take away some of the toys. At under a year, a baby's attention span is about three seconds—I think the world's record is two minutes—so when she gets bored with a toy, remove it first and then add a new toy. That should give you enough time in the kitchen—if you stick with Minute Rice.

Should we go away overnight without the baby?

The first chance you get.

#216 *After several months of motherhood, I truly believe I have bitten off more than I can chew. Will I ever feel comfortable in this role?*

Yes, you will, *if* you give up any preconceived notions about what motherhood is *supposed* to be and create your own role of motherhood that makes *you* comfortable. New mothers are suddenly thrust into what has been described as feeling like "the longest baby-sitting job in history." It just never ends. You're "on call" 24 hours a day, seven days a week, week after week, month after month. Some mothers thrive on this experience, and others are totally overwhelmed by it. Most likely, you fall somewhere in between.

What can you do? Stop paying attention to articles, talk shows, friends, and even books that try to tell you how you "should" feel. Start taking a little better care of yourself when you feel overwhelmed: get a sitter, catch a movie, get your nails done, lunch with friends—anything to break the routine. That little bit of separation will make you appreciate your role as mom a lot more when you get home.

Although you are a mother forever, you won't have to "mother" forever. If you give yourself the opportunity to be *you* first and a parent second, you'll be okay, but that's a very tough thing to do. Shoot for a wholesome compromise. It'll help.

My sister-in-law begins every sentence with, "When my kids were little—" Any good responses before I turn this one over to Dear Abby?

I think that's so wrong. You know what kind of people they are? They're the kind of people who, when they haven't seen you in a long time, say, "Hey, did you put on weight?" They come to me and say, "Hey, are you still losing your hair, doc?" I used to have a friend who did that—always compared our kids to theirs. One day, I finally told him, "You know, I don't give a damn." And you know, he never did it again.

#218 *I had my cat before I had my husband and certainly before this baby. Do I have to get rid of him (the cat) now?*

You may be referring to that old wives' tale about a cat sucking the breath out of a baby. The truth is *any* animal that has been alone with you for any length of time cannot be trusted alone with the baby. A cat will become a very big mother and will try to get into the crib—even a big German shepherd will try to get into the crib, and that's how you lose a baby—she gets smothered. That doesn't mean you have to get rid of the pet, but it does mean you have to keep a close eye on him with regard to the baby.

I've heard it's particularly dangerous to shake infants (like when you're angry).

Never, never, never shake the baby. Though the soft spot in their head, called the fontanel, is open, which does provide some protection from injury, there is still enough space between the brain and the bones of the skull—even though they're soft—so that if you shake the brain hard enough it can cause bleeding inside and brain damage. *Never, never, never shake the baby.*

Sometimes I get so angry and frustrated, it's frightening.

Yes, that can happen, especially if the baby has been keeping you up all night and you're terribly, terribly fatigued. Those feelings are normal! But when you do feel that way, walk out of the room for a few minutes, until you calm down. Never pick the baby up and shake him. Don't even go in the room if you're that angry.

What about playfully throwing the baby up in the air?

I used to do it. Once I missed my daughter, Karen, on the way down. I don't think there's anything wrong with it as long as you don't throw the baby 10 feet in the air and fail to catch him. It is not the same as shaking. Just use common sense *whenever* you're playing with the baby. (By the way, Karen just got the wind knocked out of her. She's fine now.)

What's the most common mistake grandparents make?

Believing that this is their second chance at raising a child. What they seem to forget is that this is *your* child, and you want to raise your child the way you want—not necessarily the way you were raised by your mother, even if she raised you well. Different gene pool, different lifestyle, different child.

Do grandparents often spoil the kids?

All the time. Often it is because they don't see them all the time, and they feel they have to give them material things so that they will remember them. If they just pat them on the head and say I love you, the average baby and toddler won't remember, but if you bring a favorite doll or truck, they'll remember that. My mother was the greatest example of that who ever lived. If my mother-in-law brought the kids two presents each, my mother would go out and get an extra present for each kid just to stay even. I don't think it's Jewish, Chinese, Italian, or anything else. I think the tendency is inherent in all grandparents, whether or not they act on it. These days, grandparents look forward to taking their grandchildren to ball games and theater, and that's all good stuff to share—much better than just staying in the house, baby-sitting like the old days.

Can I get appropriate health care for my baby if I'm in an HMO?

Yes. You have to go to an office that treats you as a person and not a number. They may be getting harder to find, but you have to keep looking. As the patient, you have to resist the temptation of coming into the office with a chip on your shoulder about your managed coverage, as if you're not a worthy person. If you find it's the office staff that has this kind of attitude, discuss it with the doctor. If the doctor's attitude is the same, find another doctor. Trying to understand the changes in medicine today will help. The patients no longer control their choice of doctors, and doctors no longer are entirely free to choose how to treat. The insurance company is our "big brother"; managed health care is about managing costs, not care. To have the most successful relationship, keep the lines of communication open between yourself, the doctor, and her staff.

#225 *My husband thinks that certain chores are "mom things," especially when it comes to changing diapers.*

I think some new fathers are reticent because they don't feel confident about their ability to care for the baby, but like everything else, it just takes a little practice. Unfortunately, I don't know of any way to motivate a completely unmotivated father to participate. But dads who do not involve themselves in every part of taking care of their baby are really cheating themselves out of a wonderful experience.

At a party not long ago, Leslie saw Steve *finally* changing 20-month-old Jason's rather pungent diaper. "It's about time," she said.

"What are you talking about?" asked Steve. "It says that the diapers hold *up to 40 pounds* right on the package!"

#226 *How realistic is a "Mr. Mom"? How long does that last?*

You see these guys breathe hard with their wives in labor and coach them through delivery, and they go home and help take care of the baby for a few days or even a couple of weeks, depending on their jobs. Then they have to go back to work and it's no more "Mr. Mom." It's now dad. So it's really all in how you see your role in the family and how you define it.

There are some men, however, who do successfully take on the role of primary caregiver while their wives go back to work. These guys generally get more applause than full-time moms simply because it's a more unusual role to play. The truth is that anyone who takes care of children should be applauded because it ain't easy! With any luck, whether or not there is a nonworking parent in the household, sharing the responsibilities of parenting will greatly contribute to sharing the joy.

#227 *I can't get the baby to go to sleep in the crib. Is it okay to let him fall asleep in the living room, then transfer him later?*

Where a child falls asleep is much like sleep itself. It's a habit. If the baby gets used to his crib—even if it takes a few minutes of crying to accomplish that (his, not yours)—it will be worth it in the long run.

A jovial man named Joe recently told a group of parents that none of his kids falls asleep in bed. "I've been carrying them to bed for the last 10 years," he boasted.

George, father of three, remarked, "Boy, will *you* be in great shape by the time they're 18!"

#228 *Do you think parents should learn infant CPR?*

Most definitely. Cardiopulmonary resuscitation is a life-saving procedure. Most hospitals in the United States now offer courses in CPR. Check with your local hospital or with your pediatrician. It's a very good course to take.

My six-month-old is going through some uncomfortable teething. How do you feel about zwieback, bagels, and teething rings?

I love bagels and at 64 I still like zwieback. I think plastic teething rings filled with water can be dangerous. Many parents like to freeze the teething rings because the baby likes to suck on them to numb their gums. But they defrost in the baby's mouth. If she has a sharp tooth coming out, the teething ring can burst, and she can choke. It's happened only once in my 32 years of practice, but that's enough for me. Zwieback is good but it's messy. Frozen bagels are less messy and feel good on the gums.

#230 *My seven-month-old has suddenly become a mama's girl, clinging 24 hours a day. What can I do?*

One reason that seven-month-olds are naturally fearful is that they've started to move from one point to another on their own—without you. While they're enjoying their newfound mobility, their idea of security is being attached to you, so they'll follow you from one place to another so they can be near you. And, of course, they want to be held all the time. I suggest that you put the baby in a playpen. Some people feel that a playpen is like a jail, but I disagree. There's nothing wrong with a playpen for a kid to learn how to entertain herself, although it's hard to start at seven months. If you start using the playpen early, it's less likely to become just a big toy receptacle in your living room. Plus, it keeps the baby safe when you have to run to answer the phone, cook dinner, or use the bathroom.

While most babies will go through a temporary clingy phase, those who are used to being physically apart from mom at least once in a while have less of a tendency to become "cling-ons" for any length of time.

#231 *Suddenly my very independent baby seems to be afraid of people. Is this normal?*

Yes. Somewhere between five months and nine months, babies develop stranger anxiety. Every time they see a stranger—sometimes it can even be their father who they don't see all day long—they may scream or cry. Grandparents who used to get smiles now get only a trembling lower lip. And that's very normal.

By the time they're two, they just scream when they see me, even away from my office. This is a true story. A lot of my patients have season tickets to UCLA basketball games, as I do. One night, four or five patients spotted me and brought their kids over in turn, all decked out in UCLA outfits, who were told to "say hi to Dr. Buddy." Each one screamed so loud, half of Pauley Pavilion turned around to stare. Now I just wave from a distance.

How do you feel about the family bed?

The family bed is a trend that is turning into a cult issue. I am firmly against the idea of the family bed. I think people who let their kids sleep with them on a regular basis believe they have to be with their children day and night.

They feel insecure and don't have enough faith in themselves to parent during parenting hours. Plus, the family bed doesn't allow for two adults to have a normal life in their bed—to have sexual relations, to be affectionate with each other, or even have a private conversation. I think it's an invasion of privacy, and I don't think it teaches children to respect privacy.

#233 *So the baby should never be in our bed?*

Never is such a strong word. Many new mothers, especially if they're nursing, like to keep the baby in their bed during the wee, small hours so that they don't have to get out of bed to attend to the baby several times a night. Most discontinue this practice after a very short time. Nobody is suggesting that an occasional family cuddle in a warm, toasty bed is inappropriate. However, heed this warning: When a baby gets used to sleeping with her parents, it's very, very difficult to get that baby to sleep in her own bed. It's a problem that's much easier to avoid in the first place than to correct later on.

#234 *But won't the baby feel more secure knowing the parents are near?*

If God had wanted the baby to be attached to you forever, He wouldn't have required the umbilical cord to be cut. Many people have a hard time emotionally cutting the cord and physically separating from the baby. But remember this: Your baby's security is created when you hold him in your arms, talk to him, smile at him, tell him you love him, and feed him—and as he gets through the first year, that's what's important. He recognizes your voice, he recognizes your touch and even how you smell. That's what makes him secure—not necessarily sleeping with you in your bed.

But it won't physically hurt the baby, right?

There is a danger that we didn't mention, and that's the danger of the baby suffocating when you roll over. Many people rationalize that they're sure they would awaken if they rolled over on the baby. But these tragedies occur every day, and they're so, so easy to avoid. Don't sleep with the baby.

#236

My baby has been going to day care successfully for a few months now. All of a sudden, he's causing scenes when I have to leave. Is this normal?

Yes, it's very normal. As he gets older, he's becoming more aware of being without you. If it continues for a long period of time, you have to look to see if there's something or someone at day care he's fearful of. However, at under a year, a baby can get upset about being separated from somebody who cares for him. It's very normal.

#237

Now that the baby is fully on the bottle, can I put one in his crib with him when he goes to sleep?

Absolutely, if it's *water*. You don't want to get the baby used to eating in the middle of the night, so I would avoid formula or milk. Besides, he doesn't need the extra calories.

#238 *I remember being told something about a bottle in the crib not being good for the teeth.*

That's when it contains apple juice. Don't give a juice bottle to the baby in the crib. If juice sits in the mouth when the teeth are coming in, the juice could stain the teeth. And it's full of sugar, which is bad for the teeth as well. But if it's water, I think putting a bottle in the crib is great. But just water. My grandfather gave me chicken soup in the middle of the night—and I still get up looking for chicken soup.

At what point do I switch from formula to milk?

Talk about controversy. I have many, many children who have now graduated from college who I put on low-fat milk at six weeks of age and they did just fine. Sometimes I did that because I didn't feel the babies needed the butterfat. Or if they were spitters, low-fat milk sometimes stopped the spitting. Or if they started food at an early age, they didn't need the calories in formula. Where's the controversy? Well, if I owned the laboratories that produced baby formula, I'd want babies on formula forever and would try to get word out as best I could. But I just don't think it's necessary. Talk to your pediatrician. In young babies, the gastrointestinal tract may not be ready to accept it, and the milk will not agree with the baby. However, I have had countless babies who have started on milk at under six months of age and have done very well. So allow your doctor to help you decide when your baby is able to tolerate the change.

#240 *Does he need whole milk or can I use low fat?*

Low fat is fine. Anyway, 2% low fat isn't so low fat, we're finding out.

#241 *How much fruit juice can she have during the day?*

Unless you live in an exceptionally warm climate, an infant under a year old doesn't need to have more than 32 ounces of liquid a day, including juice. However, this is a rule you can bend a little bit. If she has 32 ounces of milk or formula a day, and you add 8 ounces of juice as a snack, that's okay. Just remember that the juice should not be a substitute for milk or formula.

#242 *Is any kind of juice okay?*

I prefer the 100 percent juices because babies don't need all the extra sugar in "juice drinks." There are several varieties to choose from. In addition, I ask moms to stay away from citrus juices—no orange or grapefruit juice before 9 or 10 months—because of the frequency of allergic responses to citrus in new babies.

Should I dilute the juice?

Diluting the juice is a great idea because it cuts the sugar. Start with half water/half juice. Gradually decrease the amount of water as the baby gets used to the taste. If you have an especially heavy juice drinker, I see no problem in continuing to "cut" the juice with water indefinitely (even into the second and third year).

#244

What about water as extra fluid?

Water is really good, and most people forget about giving the baby water to drink. But remember, the easiest thing for a baby to do is to suck on a bottle. The more fluid the baby drinks, the less he will be interested in eating solid food.

How long does that 32-ounce rule of thumb apply?

Until they're seven, eight, or nine months old. By that time, they're fully on solid food and the liquid—formula or juice—is really a supplement.

My husband wants to have outings only as a family. He doesn't realize that taking the baby along every single time is no break for mom. I've tried to tell him, but he just won't listen.

Leave him with the baby for an entire day. Then have the conversation with him while he's trying to recover! Seriously, he needs to understand that your time as a family is broken up into four parts: You need time alone, he needs time alone, you need to be alone as a couple, and you need to spend time together with the baby. If he steadfastly refuses to spend time alone with you, it may be indicative of a problem that has nothing to do with the baby. Keep the lines of communication open and encourage him to tell you how he feels. Don't forget the baby has changed your lives forever, and that can be difficult for a new dad as well as a new mom.

#247

Sometimes as a timesaver, I hand my daughter to my husband in the shower. At what point should this be discontinued?

This practice should be discontinued under the following conditions:

1. Your daughter has developed the ability to point and laugh.

2. She finds she needs something to grab on to to keep from falling down.
3. She opens the shower door and says, "Hi, shorty."

Actually, I see no problem showering with a baby of the opposite sex during the first year *unless* this practice creates discomfort for either parent. And I'm guessing that one of you is uncomfortable if you're asking this question at all.

I'm a perfectionist and I really want to have a "perfect" child. Am I in for trouble?

There is no such thing as the perfect child. And that's okay, because there's no such thing as the perfect parent. The trouble perfectionist parents often run into comes from becoming what I call a "consuming parent"—one who is totally preoccupied with every single thing their child does. While new parents do need to make certain decisions for their babies—how much to eat, what to wear, where or where not to crawl—even very little babies need to make some choices on their own. If you become a perfection-seeking, consuming parent, making all the choices for your child as he grows, you're in for a big disappointment, because *no* child is perfect. Many adults can tell you the effect parents who aspired to perfection can have throughout the child's life and into adulthood. Remember, if you can keep from "consuming" the infant, you won't confuse loving and caring with overparenting.

#249 *Do I have to wash baby clothes in a special soap?*

I don't think so. It's important for you to wash any clothes before you put them on the baby, but I think you can use your own detergent, unless the baby has exceptionally sensitive skin. Then you can look for all those Ivory Snow and Dreft coupons you clipped. People who do start out washing the clothes in special detergent probably keep it up only until the end of the box. By then you'll be tired of doing separate laundry anyway, and you'll throw all the family's clothes in together. If you want a rule of thumb, the first three or four months is when the baby's skin is the most sensitive.

Should I use special bath soap for the baby?

Yes. There are many wonderful baby soaps on the market. My particular favorite, if anyone should ask, is Neutrogena Baby Soap.

#251 *How often are the scheduled doctor visits during the first year?*

This may depend on your health plan. If you have managed health care, the insurance company will probably cover visits at two months, four months, six months for immunization, nine months, and then a year. I prefer to see the baby every month for the first six months, then once at eight, ten, and twelve months. I feel it's unfair to both parents and the baby for a pediatrician not to be available for answering questions and being supportive on a regular basis, because that's what I know a pediatrician is supposed to be. Available and affable.

When does immunization start?

Actually, it can start in the hospital nursery with the first Hepatitis B vaccine (although some pediatricians opt to give it in the office at two weeks). Then we start with the DPT (diphtheria, pertussis or whooping cough, and tetanus), HIB to protect the infant against spinal meningitis (these two shots can now be combined), plus the oral polio vaccine at two, four and six months.

#253 *What do you do about diarrhea if it's not associated with other symptoms?*

If the baby has one loose bowel movement, don't get excited. Remember that the color and consistency can change from day to day and movement to movement, and a baby may have as many as 1 1/2 loose stools per feeding. If he has more than that, he may be reacting to something in mom's milk or an infection. The bottle-fed baby may be reacting to bad formula or something new in his diet.

In any case, an infant who has diarrhea in the first one to three months of life *can* become dehydrated very quickly, especially if he is having squirty, watery stools every hour or so. The younger the infant, the more careful you must be about his fluid intake and output. In fact, it's a good idea to keep track of how much the baby takes and how much diarrhea he has, because the doctor will ask you.

If you think the baby is reacting to something in mom's breast milk, avoid that food and the diarrhea should go away. You also might consider stopping breast-feeding for 12 to 24 hours. *The most important thing is to replace the fluid in the baby's system.*

What to Do

1. Find the source of the diarrhea, if at all possible, and eliminate it.

2. Check for signs of dehydration and if present, *seek help immediately.* (See Question 255.)
3. Ask your doctor to recommend a medication to stop the diarrhea.
4. Begin replacing fluids.
5. Restrict the baby's diet to water, Pedialyte, Gatorade, rice, clear broth, and banana until the baby has normal stools for two days. Ask the doctor if a stool culture is necessary.

What's the best way to replace the fluids?

If the baby has been vomiting, wait for the vomiting to stop (or consult your doctor about suppositories to accomplish this). Give *nothing* by mouth for two to three hours, then begin with one to two teaspoons of Pedialyte, Gatorade, or a mixture of Pedialyte and 7-Up, and begin replacement therapy *slowly*—every 15 minutes for one hour, gradually increasing the amount of liquid by a teaspoon or so each 15 minutes for the second and, if necessary, third hour. No matter how much the infant appears to want, *go slow.* It will take up to four hours for the stomach to tolerate even small amounts of liquid. What you want to see as replacement therapy continues is a cessation of vomiting, a perkier baby, and especially a wet diaper. Then you will know that the threat of dehydration is over.

If the baby has diarrhea but *no* vomiting, you still need to replace fluids, but there is no need to wait for the stomach to settle down, and there is no need to give fluids so slowly. Go ahead and give a bottle of Pedialyte, Gatorade, or water. What you're trying to do is to replace the fluids in his body as he is losing them through diarrhea. What you're looking for in this situation is the slowing and eventual cessation of the diarrhea and a change in consistency, from watery to a bowel movement with some substance.

What are the signs of dehydration?

If there has been vomiting and/or diarrhea associated with a high fever, watch for:

1. Decreased urine output—a long time between wet diapers. (*Note:* Today's high-absorbing disposable diapers may be soaking up a lot of urine.)
2. Dry mouth—feel the inside of his mouth.
3. No tears.
4. Pinch the skin on the stomach. If it stands up like dough, severe dehydration is present.
5. Lethargy—infant is difficult to arouse.
6. Sunken eyes.

If these symptoms are present, CALL YOUR DOCTOR OR GO TO THE EMERGENCY ROOM.

#256

How can I tell if it's something in my milk that is causing diarrhea or upset stomach?

The most common culprits are caffeine, chocolate, green vegetables, spicy foods, and overeating. All these things can cause colicky pain, diarrhea, spitting up and/or vomiting. Eliminate these and see if the baby's symptoms go away.

How can I know if the formula has gone bad if it doesn't smell bad?

If the baby gets ill with vomiting and/or diarrhea, there is a possibility that the formula has gone bad. Either it was out too long in the heat or was somehow contaminated.

Remember, with vomiting and/or diarrhea, *the possibility of rapid dehydration is strong*. Take appropriate measures.

#258

Do I always give Tylenol for fever?

No. You do not give Tylenol, or any medicine by mouth, if the fever is associated with vomiting. That's when you check with your doctor, who may direct you to fever suppositories or may want to see the baby right away.

How do I know how to give it for things other than fever?

Consult your pediatrician. Whenever you have any questions about *any* medications, consult your pediatrician.

#260

I need to call the exterminator, but two guys gave me two different stories about keeping the baby out of the house. What should I do?

Keep the baby out of the house for at least 24 hours. It is possible that some of the spray can get into air pockets in closets in the baby's room or in the room where the baby plays. That stuff could be very dangerous to a baby's blood and lungs.

#261

How did my baby get to be a food stuffer?

The parent has to be the one to say, "I stuffed him because he cried and it kept him quiet; because it made me happy to see round, fat cheeks; because he acted hungry and made sucking noises; because he was reaching for his food; and because I love him."

We're having the inside of the house painted, and I'm concerned about paint fumes and lead. What should I do?

They don't use lead in paint anymore, but if you're in an old house and scraping old paint, take the baby out. Regarding paint fumes: If the fumes give *you* a headache, they're probably giving the baby a headache. So when you paint inside, take the baby out.

We're having the outside of the house painted, and I'm concerned about the baby's safety. Anything I should keep in mind?

Just remember, you can't trust a baby once he is mobile. You can't take your eyes off of him for even a second. Watch out for the ladder. Watch out for the paint and paint thinner. If you're doing the painting yourself, have someone come in to watch the baby, or let grandma take him for the day so that there is no way he's going to get into trouble.

My eight-month-old screams when we leave the house, but my baby-sitter reports that soon after we leave, the baby's just fine. Should I worry?

Absolutely not. Infants, as they get older, get smarter, wiser, and more aware of their environment. They now know what "going out" means, and they don't want you to leave; they also know that the "scene" they create is an incredibly manipulative weapon if you allow it to change your plans. Grit your teeth, give her a kiss, and leave her in capable hands. Most of all, don't let the scene ruin your well-deserved time away. The baby will have a fine time and, hopefully, so will you.

Are baby swimming lessons a waste of money, or will it help to make the baby water-safe?

There's no such thing as "water-safe." Babies don't drown *only* because they don't know how to swim. They drown because they slip, hit their heads, and sink to the bottom when no one's around. I think the decision to give babies swimming lessons is a personal one. As a doctor, I'm not a big fan of swimming lessons in the first year because babies' sinuses aren't fully developed, and the water can cause swimmer's ear and ear infections. If you want to take a baby into the pool with you during the first year, great. Let her splash and play, but try to keep her head above water as much as possible.

#266 *When does the baby need shoes?*

When he begins to stand up and walk holding on to the furniture, he needs shoes to offer some minimal protection for feet against foreign bodies on the floor and from painful toe stubbing. When he's walking alone, he needs a little better shoe to offer him more support.

What kind of shoes? The hard baby shoes?

Any high-top tennis shoe will do. The biggest waste of money, in my opinion, is the high-top white shoe that used to be so popular. They need to be polished at least five times a day, and babies outgrow them in about two weeks. So try an inexpensive tennis shoe that can offer a baby protection when you go to the park or the beach.

One mother came to the office with her four-month-old, who was wearing those little beige hiking boots. While these boots were as cute as the devil, the baby was at the age when kids are constantly kicking their feet. "Don't those boots hurt when he kicks you?" I asked in all earnestness. I was answered by a look that said this was the dumbest question she'd been asked all day. And it was. She had the bruises to prove it.

#268 *Is helping the baby to walk a good thing, or should she be allowed to do it by herself?*

I don't think helping her hurts at all, and I don't think it will help her walk any faster. The human nervous system has never been rushed in its entire existence. Babies usually begin to walk between 11 and 15 months. If your pediatrician has been keeping an eye on your baby's development, he will alert you if there is any reason for concern. Having an early or late walker is nothing you can control, and it's certainly nothing to worry about. Just be aware that the nervous system develops at its own pace, and the overall development of the baby shouldn't be measured on the basis of any one developmental milestone, but on her progress on the whole.

#269 *Is the air conditioner and/or heater okay for the baby?*

Absolutely. Try to maintain one temperature where the baby is comfortable and you don't have to worry about several clothing changes during the day—not due to the temperature anyway. (There are other reasons babies' clothes are changed, sometimes several times during the day, as all new mothers will learn.)

#270 *Should morning and afternoon naps continue for the whole first year?*

Not necessarily. It depends on the baby. One great reason for continuing naps is so that you have some time to yourself. If he doesn't sleep, it's okay, as long as he learns to play by himself during "nap" time. An hour or two in the morning and an hour or two in the afternoon gives you a two- to four-hour respite to rest or take care of things you need to do.

What causes hiccups?

Hiccups occur when air is swallowed, which swells the stomach and presses on the diaphragm.

Any remedies for hiccups?

Sometimes before you can think of a remedy, the baby will spit up because the stomach has been so full, and that will cure the hiccups. Sometimes a sip of water or chamomile or herb tea will do it. Don't try scaring him—it won't work. He'll probably cry, and he'll still have the hiccups.

#273 *What if the baby has hiccups several times a day?*

Then you have to look and see what *you're* doing that may be causing the hiccups. It's probably not something that's wrong with the baby. Is he crying while you're feeding him, which would make him swallow air? Are you overfeeding the baby or feeding him too fast? (Check the nipple on the bottle—the hole may be too big. Change nipples.)

What medications should I keep on hand at all times?

1. Liquid Tylenol
2. Liquid ibuprofen (Advil or Motrin); use for fevers over 102 degrees
3. Tylenol suppositories (in case the baby is vomiting and can't keep Tylenol or Advil down)
4. A humidifier (which I consider a medicine)
5. Decongestant to help dry up a mild cold
6. Pediatric cough medicine for a mild cough
7. Over-the-counter cortisone cream for resistant rashes
8. Neosporin to heal the skin quickly (mix a little on your fingertip with cortisone cream, and it does a great job on diaper rashes)

9. Ipecac to induce vomiting if toxic substances are ingested
10. Pedialyte to help prevent dehydration after bouts with diarrhea or vomiting

#275 *Is there anything I can do for the baby's cold?*

A cold is going to last 7 to 12 days, no matter what we do. A little Tylenol should keep the baby comfortable and a humidifier may help keep his nose clear. Most of the things that we as physicians tell people to do is to just get the baby through that 7- to 12-day period that the cold lasts. If, however, the baby had a clear runny discharge from his nose that becomes thick and discolored, accompanied by a fever, and if he's doing a lot of crying and pulling and/or hitting his ears, contact your doctor because you may be looking at your infant's first middle ear infection. Remember, if the baby has a fever, it should *not* be attributed to teething. Fever is a sign that there is an infection brewing. Always take into consideration how the "whole child" looks in addition to identifying his symptoms.

#276 *How early does a baby learn manipulative behavior?*

As quickly as he recognizes a response to a cry, who responds, and how the person responds. What most people don't realize is that that begins to happen immediately on coming home from the hospital. More parents than you would believe are wound around those tiny, tiny pinkies in those first weeks because of the way they respond to a cry, a whimper, even a noise. Give yourself time to learn what the infant's various noises mean—otherwise, your responses will lead to the manipulative behavior.

#277 *Should the house be kept quiet while the baby sleeps?*

No. Babies sleep through music, television, dogs barking, and fire engine sirens in the driveway. I don't know when that stops. I wish I could do that now.

#278 *I realize I shouldn't pick up the baby as soon as she starts to cry, but that's how I know she's awake. When should I pick her up?*

It takes every parent a while to learn what the cries mean: I'm hungry, I'm uncomfortable, I'm wet. You can't put that in a book, you can't put that in a videotape—it just takes some time. If you give the baby a moment and she stops crying, just go about your business and don't pick her up at all for a few minutes. If you pick up a happy, gurgling baby, you are giving positive reinforcement to that desired behavior, and it follows that the baby will learn to be happy and gurgle more and more. Pretty soon, when she wakes up she'll think, "Hello, I'm awake, where is everyone? Well, they all must be busy. I'll just have to wait a little longer in here until they come . . . or I get hungry—then I'll let them know I'm awake!"

#279 *My baby won't lie down in the crib to go to sleep. Should I leave him standing there?*

Absolutely. This often happens between six and nine months, when the "white-knuckle syndrome" sets in. That's when the baby knows how to pull up and hold on to the crib rail, but he doesn't know how to make his fingers let go so he can lie down. So he'll just stand there and scream and scream! Finally, he'll let go and when you go into the room, he's sound asleep. But if you get him accustomed to your going in and undoing those white knuckles, that's what he's going to expect every time. This is the kind of addictive response on your part that can lead to manipulative behavior.

I don't want to leave my husband out, but my priorities have definitely changed since the baby was born. How do I keep our relationship the way it was?

As you know, there are books written about this subject and even courses taught, but here are my two cents. Sure your priorities have changed, but you've got to make your husband a priority, too. Remember, this kid won't always want to be with you, as she develops her own relationships within her own society, beginning with the first day of preschool. Your husband is supposed to be your best friend. Treat him that way. Give the relationship with your husband the attention it deserves. If you make your husband a priority, he's more likely to understand when the baby takes up so much of your time and energy. The truth is, if your relationship is okay, the baby is going to be just fine. It's the consuming parents whose entire existence revolves around that baby, day and night, who wind up having a pretty awful relationship with each other.

#281 *How can I keep our relationship lively when I'm always dead tired?*

First, you have to remember that once you have a child, your relationship is forever, ever, ever changed. It will *never* be the same. Things that were done with a great deal of spontaneity are not going to be done. Things that you could do on a moment's notice, like go to the movies, you can't do anymore. Forget having sex on the kitchen table. But if you're continually too tired to be lively, it's because *you're* not in control. The baby is controlling your life. Now, if you're tired at the very beginning, that's normal. However, after about three months, under normal circumstances, the baby should be sleeping six to seven hours during the night. And that should be enough for you to start getting back to some normal routine, like having a relationship with your husband. You've got to take control of the fatigue factor. It's your life, you get only one shot at it. Make your priorities and let the baby fit into your lifestyle. Your entire family will be happier, and I believe healthier, for this practice.

My husband and I have had arguments about my interfering when he's taking care of the baby. I can't help it. If I think he's doing something wrong, I just have to step in.

What's the most a husband can do wrong? Put the diaper on wrong? Put the shirt on backward? Put on clothes that don't match? What difference does that make? It may be true that some fathers don't know how to clean up a baby real well when changing a dirty diaper—so you'll clean up the baby in a little while. If you want the father to be involved, let him go for it. Obviously, if you see him doing something that is specifically unsafe for the baby, I'm sure he'll thank you for pointing it out to him. Tactfully.

Save the arguments for the second year, when you may start to disagree on discipline.

I need to have the carpets cleaned. Will the chemicals affect the baby?

Yes. They can affect the baby by skin contact as well as through the respiratory system. Keep the baby away from the newly cleaned carpets for 24 hours, just to be safe.

#284 *Sometimes he makes me so mad I could scream! And I do! How can I stop myself?*

All children, even very young babies, can be exasperating at times. This goes with the territory. My advice is to just walk away before it becomes an explosive situation. This accomplishes two things. First, you get the chance to cool off—which will be ultimately better for the baby—and second, you deprive the baby of an audience for his bad behavior—which makes it much less fun to do.

One of my moms has one kid in preschool and an 11-month-old. She told me that the older child frequently reported to her that he had been given a "time-out" in school that day for whatever major or minor infractions he had committed. That term stuck in her mind, and the next time she found herself flipping out at her kids, she announced, "Mommy is taking a five-minute time-out!" and she planted herself in a chair across the room. The kids were so startled, they left her alone, and she had time to cool off. Not a bad idea!

#285 *I want to make sure I'm getting my baby girl clean when I change her, but how do I know?*

Baby girls have more creases and crevices than little boys. Always remember to clean from top to bottom, *not* bottom to top, so as not to contaminate the vagina and urethra with fecal material. And, later on, that's how you have to teach a little girl to wipe herself, too.

Do babies dream?

Sure they do. Everyone who sleeps dreams, because the brain is never really asleep.

#287 *Do babies remember their dreams?*

I don't know. I've asked several, but I've never gotten an answer. But you can be sure that in the near future, scientists will find a way to know about babies' dreams, and I'm sure what we learn will be fascinating.

Can small babies have nightmares?

Yes, and I've always thought that their first nightmare is about me. Actually, babies who are hospitalized in the first year and suffer from pain and needles and the separation from their parents often have a well-founded fear of doctors. Babies who are sick a lot and have to go to the doctor often do have real fears, and I think fears occasionally manifest themselves in their bad dreams—even for babies. Most nightmares, however, begin during the second year and usually occur sometime before midnight.

How can I keep the baby from becoming fearful?

Most of the fears that babies have, they get from us. If we jump at noises, they're going to jump at noises. If we react with a scream at certain things, that's what babies are going to do. And if every time the baby falls, we run to pick him up, that can create a fear, too. Babies freefall when they're under a year old, so the chances of them badly hurting themselves are very small. Now, I'm not talking about them falling from a table or the crib onto the floor, but falling down as they're learning to pull themselves up and walk the furniture. If you're a mom who says, "Ooo-ooo-ooo" every time the baby falls, and picks him up and makes a fuss, falling down is what he will do to get that attention from you.

I had a mother who gave her kid a sugar cube to make him feel better every time he fell down. Now, under those circumstances, a smart kid would fall down a lot! She said, "How do I keep him from falling? He falls all the time!" When she told me how she used the sugar cube, she answered her own question.

We dealt with a lot of fear after the big California earthquake a few years ago, fear on the part of the parents being passed along to the kids. I'll tell you one thing, if you've got to be in an earthquake, be under a year old. You'll just think it's like the car rocking, and it won't really bother you.

#290 *I don't want to sound negative to the baby, but I find myself saying no about a thousand times a day. I'm even tired of hearing it! Any suggestions?*

Do you really need to say all those no's? If you use it too much, of course it's not going to be effective or get the baby's attention. Try making a list of what you say no to. I asked a mother to do this, and her list contained 546 no's. I said, "Barbara, see if you can't cut it down to 450 no's!"

We laughed and laughed, but when she came in the next time, she had cut it down to 450. She kept the list. What she found out was that with half the stuff she said no to, it wasn't effective because (1) the baby was too busy doing whatever he was doing to hear her, and (2) there wasn't any good reason to say no—it was just that she reacted to every little thing he did. This all took place when her son was about eight months old, and that's when you find yourself saying no all the time.

Saying no can really become a habit as children get older, and creating that list will be even more helpful when the kids are two, three, and four years old.

#291 *I realize babies should develop at their own pace, but is there anything I can do to stimulate either emotional or motor development?*

Personally, as a physician who has been in practice for 33 years, I am not in favor of pushing the kids to develop earlier and faster. The "Mommy & Me" classes are great for mommy, but if you're there to educate that baby, you're in the wrong pew. A nervous system develops at its own pace.

An emotional system, however, is something different. Frankly, I think a new mother or father would be better off spending time developing his or her own identity and emotional maturity for this reason: *You* develop the baby's emotional well-being on a daily basis by feeding and cuddling and talking lovingly—and if *you* are on an even keel emotionally, your baby will develop just fine. Your maturity as a parent, and your level of patience, is directly related to your ability to rear your child.

The process of parenting is a constant learning experience. Be patient with yourself as well as with the baby.

What's the difference between a vaporizer and a humidifier?

A humidifier creates a cool mist; a vaporizer, a hot mist. A cool mist has been my choice over a number of years because when an infant has a fever, the cool air feels much better than the hot air put out by a vaporizer. My years of hospital experience have taught me that the coolness liquefies the thick mucus quicker, and if the infant has a fever, she will do better in the cool environment of this homemade "tent."

Do I really need either one?

Yes. A humidifier is a good thing to have in the house. Eventually, your baby may have trouble sleeping when he's congested, and the humidifier will help him breathe better and sleep better. And rather than run around to all-night pharmacies looking for a humidifier in the middle of the night, have one in the house, ready when you need it.

How do you feel about walkers?

I believe they're unsafe. I think they're totally unnecessary, and the American Academy of Pediatrics wants them off the market. They tip over, they fall down stairwells, they bump into tables, they're just not safe. Plus, they don't help your baby walk sooner, or better, or anything. Yet many parents say their babies absolutely love walkers, and they're still being sold every day. If you do decide to use one, just be aware of the safety factors and take special precautions so your baby doesn't get injured. When she is in the walker, always, always, always make sure you have safety gates engaged blocking off stairways. Toppling down the stairs is the most common way babies get hurt in walkers.

#295 *Is anyone ever satisfied about how their baby is progressing?*

Yes and no. Weight gain is the most significant progress note parents are unhappy about. You know, it's funny. You can't wait till your baby eats solid food, then you think he eats too much. You can't wait until he crawls, and then he gets into everything. You can't wait until he talks, and then you can't get a word in edgewise. Every stage has its challenges. And it's important to remember that.

#296 *When do a baby's eyes get to be the color that they will stay?*

Sometime during the first year, when the baby acquires melanin, the body's natural pigment. I've even seen eyes that have changed color two or three times during the first year.

#297 *Well, I've tried to do it all, but I can't. I find that if I'm taking proper care of the baby and working, the house or the cooking will suffer. Do other people really do it all?*

The answer is really no, unless they have a nanny, a housekeeper, and a cook. I don't see how anyone who works full-time runs a family, too. I know it's done every day, and I have the highest regard for working mothers. Being a parent is really a full-time job. But in today's society, the reality is that in most families, both parents need to work. So, should *you* go back to work? Absolutely. Then you'll have two full-time jobs—two difficult, time-consuming, full-time jobs. The trick is to set priorities, set schedules, try your darnedest and hope for the best. Don't worry if the beds occasionally go unmade, toys accumulate in the living room, and dinner is sometimes the fast-food du jour. Being a parent is the most consuming job there is. And, by the way, the most satisfying.

#298 *My mother always said "hands up" to any baby who coughed. Does this really help?*

Yes. Actually it does. Lifting a baby's hands above her head expands the chest and lengthens the trachea, enabling the baby to either cough up whatever is in her throat or allowing it to go down.

#299 *Shall I try over-the-counter medications for the baby before bothering the doctor?*

Yes and no. It depends what you're getting medication for. If the baby has no fever and is eating reasonably well, I think going to over-the-counter medicines for a little cold is fine. If the child has had a fever for more than two or three days, or if the fever is accompanied by vomiting, diarrhea, or lethargy, you *must* talk to the doctor and not rely on over-the-counter medication.

#300 *If I am a hitter or hollerer, is it true that my child will likely be one, too?*

Yes, that is the likelihood, since statistics show that hitting begets hitting. That's because hitting is a form of control. If a parent doesn't learn to control a child by *showing,* but rather by hitting or kicking or screaming, that's what the child will learn as acceptable behavior. This can start as early as during the first year.

#301 *When are spinal taps deemed necessary?*

A spinal tap should be done to rule out meningitis. The indications are:

1. A high fever
2. Lethargy and loss of appetite with or without a fever
3. A seizure with a high fever
4. A fever, lethargy, and an increased white blood count

It is better to do a spinal tap and have it come out normal than not to do it and have a comatose infant with spinal meningitis. It is not dangerous, if done correctly, and with good reason.

#302 *When do I have to give a fever suppository?*

When your baby has been vomiting and has a temperature of 102 degrees or more. If she's unable to keep down the oral medication, a suppository is the way to get some fever-reducing medication into her body.

#303 *I am walked, rocked, and lullabyed out. What can I do to get this baby to sleep?*

Try this: Keep an inexpensive cassette recorder in the baby's room. Make a five-minute tape of mom and dad's voice talking to the baby. When you put him to bed, play the tape. He'll hear your voices talking to him in soothing, low tones and he'll go to sleep. This works just beautifully with babies who cry a lot when you try to put them down for a nap or for the night. Stop walking, stop rocking, and let the baby rock himself to sleep. I promise he will, if you can have some tolerance for a little noisy crying and the foresight to know that in the long run, what you are doing for yourself and the baby is a huge favor, as well as the right thing to do.

#304 *The baby has a continually runny nose. Is it possible he already has hay fever?*

Yes. It's possible that he has allergic rhinitis—another term for hay fever—which means he has a clear runny nose and an allergy to something in the air or in the diet. In a new baby, we try to find out what the child is allergic to—

milk, or something that you may be eating or drinking if you're breast-feeding—but as long as his nose is running clear, it's not something to worry a lot about.

What should I give him for a runny nose?

Often an over-the-counter antihistamine like Benadryl could help him greatly, if he's not too young (we really don't like to give those antihistamines to babies under two months old). Babies who require antihistamines during the first year, even over-the-counter ones, should be given them only under the watchful eye of the pediatrician.

#306

I've heard of antibiotics being given on a preventative basis. Doesn't this cause the baby to develop a tolerance to the drug?

No, not at all. We've been treating kids with antibiotics for years and years—and if a particular drug doesn't work, that particular organism isn't sensitive to the antibiotic. Quite often we'll just switch to another antibiotic until we find one that works. After helping to raise a generation of children, I can safely say that it's the organism that becomes resistant, not the host—that is, the child. Pediatricians are aware that 90 percent of all childhood diseases are viral, and so you may ask, why treat with an antibiotic? Well, for one thing, we really have no fast way to identify the virus, although the blood count and throat culture will help. Quite honestly, most of us are aware that we probably overtreat because we are afraid of secondary infections. No, this is not the holistic approach. It *is*, however, our attempt to prevent the child from getting more ill.

#307 *My baby loves to swing in his swing, but when he falls asleep, his head falls to the side. Is this at all dangerous?*

No. The heads of all sleepy infants who are too young to hold their heads erect flop over. There is nothing wrong with this. They may look uncomfortable, but they're fine.

My coauthor, Nancy, took her three-week-old baby, Ian, into a colleague's office for a brief visit. The colleague's mother arrived, saw this very tiny baby scrunched down in the infant seat, asleep with his head flopped over to the side, and demanded in a rather judgmental tone, "Is he *comfortable?*"

"He makes a living," Nancy replied.

#308 *What's the difference between a cough suppressant and an expectorant?*

A suppressant is designed to stop the cough. An expectorant tries to loosen the cough.

#309 *How do I know which to give and when?*

If the baby has a wet cough, it usually comes from a postnasal drip, as the result of a normal cold. You can use a combination antihistamine/decongestant and alternate it with a mild cough medicine. And if the baby has a dry cough that sounds like a seal barking (croupy cough), definitely call your doctor—even before you've given anything to loosen the cough—unless you've had the experience before.

#310 *At what age should the baby give up the bottle and go to a junior cup?*

If you're reading this book because your baby is under a year old, this question may not apply. You can certainly give the baby a bottle for the entirety of the first year. When she's had enough, she'll push away the bottle and take the cup. You don't want your three-year-old to walk around with a bottle hanging from her neck. As a matter of fact, it's okay to introduce the cup at any time you see fit. I've never seen evidence to the contrary.

The baby makes a lot of noise when he sleeps. Could he actually be snoring?

Yes, he probably is snoring. The baby's nose may be stuffed because he has a cold or allergy, or he may already have enlarged adenoids. More importantly, if the baby comes home like that, it's because a membrane in the back of the nose hasn't opened yet, but will open with time. If it doesn't open in two or three weeks, the doctor should be consulted.

#312 *She's too little to blow her nose. How do I clear out her nose?*

In nearly every baby gift-pack you receive, you'll see a little nose syringe. One of my moms describes it as the world's smallest turkey baster. Holding the baby's head with one hand, you can suction each nostril quickly and efficiently. You'll get much better results than holding a tissue up to her nose and saying, "Blow!"

#313 *My baby is always wet. I mean all the time. Sometimes I think he's sprung a leak.*

Usually you'll find he's sprung a leak right when you take his diaper off. That's when you have to learn to duck. If the baby seems wet all the time, that's simply because he's a baby, and the bladder muscles need time to mature. He may actually wet his diaper more than a dozen times a day. But that will decrease with time. (You'll still have to duck, though.)

#314 *Is it all right to hold my baby in my arms in the car when someone else is driving?*

No, never. By law, an infant must be driven in a car seat. (Parameters may vary from state to state; California, for example, requires the use of car seats for children under 40 pounds.) It is essential to secure the baby in a car seat every time you take him in the car, even if it's "only around the corner." In some areas, parents are being held legally liable if their child is injured, or even killed, if they're not in a car seat or safety belt. I believe that's totally appropriate.

I'm breast-feeding and I've just come down with a terrible sore throat. I'm good and sick. What should I do?

Get to your doctor for a throat culture. It's important because it can tell what you might look for in your baby. If you're congested, your doctor can give you some nasal spray to decongest your nose and an antibiotic to treat your sinuses. It's okay to take your medicine as long as it's not long acting. Take a decongestant or antibiotic or fever medicine just after you've breast-fed. You're going to be taking the medication every eight hours, and you're going to be feeding the baby every four hours, so the baby won't be feeding within four hours of your taking the medicine. The baby will be fine and so will you—in 48 to 72 hours.

This is how I would handle it, but it is very important to seek the advice of your own doctor on this particular issue.

How do you know if your baby has a sore throat?

1. Loss of appetite and a fever
2. Fever, followed by loss of appetite
3. Fever and vomiting
4. Sore throats can also be sore mouths from thrush

Most babies have a good appetite during the first year, so when the appetite suddenly changes, even if there's no fever, you've got a pretty good idea that something's going on. If it lasts more than a day, call the doctor.

#317 *My six-month-old sometimes pulls his own hair. Is this normal?*

Very normal. They find their hair. They find their toes. They find all parts of their bodies. This is how they learn. If he's pulling his hair, he's just experiencing a new texture. If he pulls his hair until it hurts, he'll stop!

#318 *Whenever I change his diaper, my baby plays with his penis. Is this because it's, ahem, pleasurable? Should I discourage it?*

Don't discourage it, it is probably pleasurable, and it may itch. In that order. It may be hard to imagine a little baby with jock itch, but they do get it because their urine dries out the skin and causes the baby to itch—so a little lotion after a bath will help greatly.

#319 *I'd like my eight-month-old to try drinking from a cup. What's the best kind?*

I'm not much in favor of those thick, nonspill training cups, rounded on the bottom, because they're heavy and they become weapons in the hands of an eight-month-old. You might try a small plastic cup that he can get his hands around and put a very little bit of liquid in it so that when he spills (not *if*, but when), neither you nor he will get too upset. Or you can use the little plastic glasses with a removable spout top or a top that has a built-in straw. Any choice you make is okay as long as the cup is lightweight.

#320 *My baby sometimes flails her arms and legs very excitedly. Could she be having some kind of seizure?*

Absolutely not. She's just excited, and these movements are very normal. When she was born, the doctor checked for the presence of the Moro reflex, a very important "startle reflex," in which babies' arms flail about as a reaction to a loud noise. But now she's just reacting to the new sights and sounds and smells that she experiences every day. As a matter of fact, having seen countless babies do this, I think they look happy, like they're free

and reaching out to the world. It is not a seizure by any means, and it does not indicate hyperactivity, at least not at this age.

Other babies seem so smiley and happy, while mine is very serious. Could my baby be unhappy?

Probably not. As long as there is a reaction to you, as a parent (in other words, he follows you with his eyes, responds to your voice, etc.), I wouldn't be too concerned. A baby's personality has to develop over time, and I don't know that you can identify a personality in a baby from day one, though many people try.

When our first baby was born, in Mexico, our housekeeper would always say he was smiling at the angels. It didn't take us long to learn that he was smiling because he passed gas.

No reaction is a warning sign. Definitely consult the doctor.

I'm afraid that if the people who take care of the baby for me—baby-sitters, day-care people, aunties and grandmas—kiss and cuddle the baby, she won't think it's special when I do it. Is this selfish?

It's certainly up to you who kisses and cuddles the baby. But do remember that an infant thrives on affection. And there's nothing in this world that will prevent her from recognizing the special kisses she gets from mom. Your special kisses, your voice, the way you hold her, and especially the communication that happens when your eyes meet hers—these things set you apart from everybody else in her life, even if she gets affection from others. You'll find out when she's a bit older that when she skins a knee or when her feelings are hurt, mom is the only one who will do.

When she was little, her bowel movements seemed effortless, to say the least. Now she strains and grunts. Is there something wrong?

No, unless the stool is hard, because this can cause small anal tears called anal fissures, which are not serious but can be painful. After babies are about two months old, their bowel movements change, especially if their diets have changed. They're eating more, they may get a little constipated from time to time, and they'll have fewer—and sometimes bigger—bowel movements than before. Often it's a question of position. If they're on their back, trying to push out a BM, they don't have the aid of gravity. They turn red and blue and purple and make all sorts of noises and sometimes push out only one little thing, something that looks like a small walnut. Makes you wonder what all the effort was about!

#324 *My baby has started to bang his head against the side of the crib. What in the world is this about? Could he be autistic?*

No. Not if his other responses are all right. Babies tend to rock back and forth because it's a motion that feels good. If he happens to be bumping his head as he rocks—trust me, when it hurts enough, he'll stop. I've never seen a baby who bangs his own head enough to cause any damage.

There is a possibility, however, that as the baby gets older, he may become a chronic head-banger. In that case, I would say the remedy is to take the mattress out of the crib and put it in the middle of the floor. Then there's nothing for him to bang his head on.

Is chickenpox dangerous under a year? What can I give him?

Not dangerous, it just makes an infant very restless because there are very few medicines we can give to help at that age. Your doctor cannot prescribe the anti-itch medicine, Periactin, that we use in older children, but an antihistamine like Benadryl is okay, in addition to Aveeno baths to make him comfortable. There's always a greater chance for infection with an infant who's crawling around and whose hands get dirty from the floor, since you can't tell a six-month-old not to scratch and expect him to understand, let alone comply. So just keep him comfortable, keep his fingernails short, and weather the storm for a few days.

Hopefully, enough people will get their children vaccinated against chickenpox—even young adults should be vaccinated—so that it becomes less common for all ages. The vaccine is called Varivax and is now available.

#326

When I decide to stop breast-feeding, can I stop all at once or should I wean the baby gradually?

Many mothers find it difficult to go "cold turkey" because when you hold the baby, he associates your feel, your smell, and your touch with getting a little snack, and that can make it difficult for you both. In addition to being difficult emotionally, it may be physically very uncomfortable; the baby's crying will often cause your breasts to leak, and if they're not emptied it may be painful. I believe that this is another very personal issue that you need to consider carefully and make your own choice.

#327 *If I go back to work, can I nurse morning and evening and have the baby take formula during the day?*

Absolutely. And as you reduce your feeding schedule, your supply of milk will also decrease accordingly, so this is a very good idea for nursing mothers who go back to work and want to continue to breast-feed.

#328 *How do I know when my baby has begun to teethe? At what age?*

When the baby begins the teething process, you'll notice an increase in the amount of saliva, a whole lot of drooling, and the desire to chew on anything and everything, including her own fist or foot. That first tooth will pop through the gums anytime between three months and about one year.

Which teeth come in first?

Once the baby has begun to teethe, the process will continue almost continually until about two years of age. The teeth will usually erupt in the following order:

1. Two lower incisors (front teeth)
2. Four upper incisors
3. Two lower incisors and all four first molars (back teeth)
4. Four canines (eyeteeth)
5. Four second molars

How can I help the process if the baby is uncomfortable?

Here are a few tips to help with teething:

1. Give her ibuprofen (Advil or Motrin). It is an anti-inflammatory that works great on swollen gums.
2. Give her a frozen bagel, a Popsicle, or a teething biscuit.

3. Massage her swollen, irritated gum with your finger for two minutes. Repeat as often as necessary.
4. Massage her gum with a small piece of ice. This will numb the area.
5. Place a wet washcloth in the freezer for 30 minutes and give it to her to suck on. It's very soothing.

These warnings bear repeating:

1. *Do not attribute a fever to teething.* You may be overlooking an infection that needs medical attention.
2. *Do not tie a teething ring around her neck.* It could catch on something or she could get her little hand caught up inside it and she could strangle.
3. *Do not* give her a frozen teething ring filled with water. It could burst and she could choke.
4. *Do not* give her hard foods (like raw carrots) to chew on that might break and cause her to choke.
5. *Do not* overuse numbing medicine. It could numb her throat and cause her to choke.

The baby sleeps great during the day, but he's restless at night. What can I do?

Try this. If the baby has napped for three hours, gently wake him and play with him or feed him. By cutting down the amount of time he sleeps during the day, you may cut down the amount of time he is awake at night. Continue this practice until he creates the habit of sleeping longer periods of time at night rather than by day. Although this sounds great in theory, I'm afraid there's no guarantee with this one.

When he is restless at night, of course you need to tend to his restlessness if he's not feeling well. But if he is okay, the nighttime restless behavior can become a habit. After checking him briefly to make sure he's all right, let him cry.

Should I send my child to day care if he's ill?

Yes and no. It's okay for him to go to day care if he has no fever, vomiting, or diarrhea. If he has a runny nose, it's okay to send him if it's running clear. If he has a fever, vomiting, or diarrhea, or if his nose is running green, keep him home.

I don't have a clue how to discontinue breast-feeding. I hope you have some tips for me!

I do have some tips, and they come by way of one of my very able nurses. Here's what she tells all the moms in our office who want to stop breast-feeding.

Milk production follows the law of supply and demand, meaning the milk that is supplied is the amount that the baby is consuming. When you decide to stop breast-feeding, the idea is to *slow* your milk production down without becoming engorged, which can sometimes be painful. Here are some steps to follow to eliminate breast-feeding while avoiding engorgement:

1. Omit one feeding. Give the baby a bottle instead.
2. When you experience the "let-down" sensation—when the milk ducts are full and milk flows into the nipple—manually express just enough milk to relieve the pressure. Then place a cold hand towel up against your breasts and fold your arms, holding the towel firmly against them for 5 to 10 minutes. Repeat this as often as needed each time you feel the "let-down" sensation. This gives your body the message to stop producing as much milk.
3. After doing this procedure for three days, omit another feeding and repeat these techniques for another three days. Replace one feeding every three days with a bottle until your baby is completely weaned.

#334

My 11-month-old catapulted from the crib and landed on the floor. I'm afraid he'll hurt himself. What should I do?

You're right, the baby can hurt himself if he continues to pole vault over the crib side onto the floor. My recommendation—and I'm not kidding—is to put a volleyball net over the crib, preventing him from catapulting out (and coming into your bed when you're asleep). Sounds a little crazy, but it works!

My baby has a reddish birthmark on her leg. Is this something that will go away?

Those reddish—almost purple—slightly raised, irregularly shaped birthmarks, made up of a collection of blood vessels, are commonly called "strawberries," and are harmless. If you really want it removed, medicine is making great strides in laser surgery, a technique which, in the near future, may make these marks disappear.

You may also have heard of "stork bites," which are flat pink birthmarks usually found over the bridge of the nose, the eyelids or on the back of the neck. These marks on the nose or eyelids generally disappear on their own before the child is two years old. Most marks on the neck also clear, but some can remain into adulthood. If "stork bites" persist, there is a good chance that laser surgery will also be used to eradicate these marks or the scars they may leave behind.

#336 Does thumb-sucking cause buck teeth?

Only if the thumb-sucking continues once the child's permanent teeth come in. Most children who are thumb-suckers as babies break the habit on their own because they are so busy with preschool and friends and so many other activities. During the first year you certainly have nothing to worry about.

#337 Can thumb-sucking hurt teeth that aren't in yet?

No. In fact the dentist we consulted thinks thumb-sucking in babies is a good thing. Since sucking is a survival instinct, thumb-sucking keeps them in good practice, she said. And, at the risk of beating a dead binkie, this particular dentist agrees with us that thumb-sucking is preferable to the use of a pacifier.

#338 *The baby loves to chew on everything, now that she's teething. Are teething rings okay as long as they're not water filled?*

Sure, but *do not tie a teething ring around a baby's neck.* I have personally known of two babies who choked when they got their little hands caught underneath the string. Do not tie *anything* around the baby's neck. Your baby can strangle.

Are numbing medicines good for the gums when teething?

Boy, those commercials are great. They show a crying baby having some medicine applied to the gums and turning immediately into a smiling, cooing cherub. What they don't tell you is that if you put on too much numbing medicine and he swallows it, he can choke. *Please, please* use this stuff very sparingly.

My baby cries for hours and hours. I'm just exhausted—and worried. What could be wrong?

Most often, colic is the answer to unexplained crying in an otherwise healthy newborn, one to three months old. The baby has no fever, no cold, no obvious source of pain. The doctor has checked for a hernia, a swollen scrotum, he finds nothing. The baby is well fed. He's fine between bouts of crying, he's fine when he's being held. But the baby may cry from one to two hours at a time, several times during the course of the day and night. Although most baby books say this usually stops by the time the baby is three months old, this is no consolation to me or to any parent going through it.

One simple solution is to take the baby for a ride. The rocking motion of the car is very soothing to babies. Pay attention to where you're going, however. I got a call one morning about 5 A.M. from a frustrated dad who said the baby had been crying for most of the previous eight hours. So I told him to take the baby for a ride. At about 9 A.M. the mom called wanting to know what I told her husband to do because he and the baby were still gone. At 11:30 A.M. dad and baby returned home. They had driven all the way to Santa Barbara from Encino, California, more than 90 miles, *but,* dad reported, the baby slept all the way home!

Another tip is to run the vacuum cleaner. Quite often the drone of the machinery will calm the baby down. Sometimes running water does the same.

Failing all else, your pediatrician may prescribe a mild antihistamine, a mild antispasmodic, or an often effective homeopathic remedy called, appropriately, "gripe water," a mixture of bicarbonate of soda, anise (which gives it a licorice taste), and another ingredient we've never quite been able to identify.

Okay, my baby's simply a crier. How do I know when there's really something wrong?

First, look at her closely and check for any obvious physical cause of pain. Don't forget to check for tight clothing, especially around the foot and the wrist. Tight clothing can cut off circulation in those chubby feet and wrists and really cause pain. Some babies even get some of their own hair wound tight around their fingers, and that can cut off circulation and hurt like hell. Give your doctor a call—

If your baby's cry is a painful one rather than a fussy one.
If she is consistently crying for two or three hours at a time.
If she is less than three months old.
If she has a fever or cold or decreased appetite.
If you are afraid you have hurt her.
If you've shaken her hard to get her to stop crying.

If there's vomiting, diarrhea, or constipation that occurs with the crying.

If you're exhausted from all this crying.

I swore I wouldn't get into this security blanket routine, but she already has a little "blankie" she clings to all the time. Should I stop making an issue of it?

Yes, absolutely stop making an issue of it. It's just not worth it. My oldest son had a security pen, of all things. We taped it, we bandaged it, he threw it out the window of the car, we stopped the car to get it. One time at the park, he threw it down the drain. I almost had to go into the sewer to get his damn pen. One day, after one of these episodes, I thought, "Hey, I'll just get him another pen." He hasn't forgotten it to this day. So when your baby is ready to get rid of the blanket, she'll get rid of it. I've even seen kids with little patches of their original blanket that they carry around, maybe two inches square. It's okay.

My baby likes the baby-sitter more than me! I'm just devastated!

This is such a common lament. Let me assure you that kids always know who their mom is, even if they go to the sitter or nanny or anyone else first. The first time most parents experience this is when the baby is six or seven months old, and they go away on a short vacation. They can't wait to get home to the baby, and when they walk in, the baby crawls right by them and goes to the sitter. It's heartbreaking, but very common.

In the interest of getting back into the world, I'd like to get my hair and nails done, but the only way I can do it is to take the baby—and it kind of smells in the beauty shop.

Taking a newborn into a beauty shop isn't a great idea. There are fumes from the hair color and the nail mixtures, and there's hair spray all over the place. Either have the baby looked after by someone in the shop who is away from all the action, or consciously keep him away from fumes and spray. If you have a hooded seat or a buggy, you can drape something over him. Excess coughing or teary eyes will tell you not to take him back into that environment again. The best idea, however, is to have someone at home stay with him and consider this an outing for yourself. You'll be able to relax much more, and the baby will be much better off.

#345 *I never thought of that. That means when I do my hair and nails at home, I should make sure the baby is out of range*

Yes, that's right. *Warning:* Not only do you have to be aware of what sprays and fumes may get into his eyes and lungs as a newborn, make sure those brightly colored spray cans are not made available to the crawling, creative 6- to 12-month-old.

Can I use the microwave to heat baby food?

Don't heat up formula in the microwave. All the literature supports the idea that injuries to infants' mouths come from overheated formula heated in the microwave. Even though you mean to be very careful, at two in the morning, you might not be as alert as you need to be to make sure the baby doesn't get a mouthful of hot formula. For the same reasons, I am not a big fan of using the microwave to heat baby food jars, but if you choose to use the microwave, be very sure to check the food carefully before feeding, *especially* the bottom of the jar and the bottom of the bottle. Different amounts and different containers can alter the temperature of the food, and it can be too, too hot. Also, be very careful that the baby doesn't get his hands on a hot jar right out of the microwave.

#347 *Now that the baby has some teeth and can sit up, can I give him any grown-up food cut up in little pieces?*

Absolutely. He should be able to pick it up with his little fat fingers.

#348 *I've heard of kids choking on hot dogs but my kid loves them. Are they really a no-no?*

People tend to slice hot dogs for the baby into little disks and that size fits great in their little hands, but it's also the perfect size to get caught in the throat. Make sure you cut up each piece into quarters—very little. *Remember,* do not leave the infant alone when you feed him something like this. Choking happens so quickly. Also, don't put too many pieces in front of him at one time. Give him a few pieces. When he's done, give him a few more.

#349

My baby never objected to bath time before, but now she just screams and screams through it every time. I don't remember her getting frightened by anything in particular. What should I do?

Sponge bathe her for a while. The idea isn't for her to take a bath, it's to get her clean, so do it any way you can. She'll become more and more accustomed to the water and will eventually get back into the bath. Many kids who scream at bath time just don't like having their movements restricted in the water, and of course it's for their own safety that you must restrict them. Once they can sit up, try a little bath seat that affixes to the tub with suction cups. Then stand back, because that's when they get to be champion splashers. But that's also when you'll begin to hear giant squeals of delight.

#350

My city gets very cold in the winter, and everywhere we go has steam heat. So we go from cold to hot to cold to hot. Is this bad for the baby?

It's not always possible to have the baby in the perfect environment, and going from cold to hot and back will make anyone's nose run, including the baby's. We even experience it in warm weather because we are constantly in and out of air conditioning, for example, going between a hot San Fernando Valley day and a cool mall. Keeping a baby's environment as constant as possible, between 70 and 74 degrees, is preferable. If you can't do that, keep the tissues at the ready. That's a pretty snotty answer, but hey—

What do I wake you up for? Can you give me a list I can keep by the phone?

It is good that you are concerned with calling your doctor in the middle of the night before the necessity arises. Personally, I want to be awakened for . . .

Difficulty breathing, including a wheezy cough or a barky cough.

A newborn with a fever.

A newborn who has had a healthy appetite and now has refused to eat two or three times in succession.

If the lack of appetite is accompanied by vomiting or diarrhea.

A sudden high fever of 103 to 105 degrees.

A fever associated with vomiting.

Anyone who goes into the field of pediatrics expects to be called in the middle of the night, so you shouldn't feel bad about calling when you need to.

#352

Since the weather has been so warm, my baby has little red dots in various places on her body, mainly the creases in her arms. What is this?

Prickly heat. Keep the baby dressed in cool clothing, and because it itches, put some nonmedicated powder on the affected area. It'll go away when the weather changes and if the baby is dressed appropriately.

Can she have fruit punch or other sweetened drinks? I'm afraid of the sugar.

Stay away from these during the first year. Otherwise, you'll never get them to eat any food. They'll choose the punch every time!

I'm just not a big fan of a lot of medication. How do you feel about homeopathic remedies?

I think that if an infant—or child or *any* human being for that matter—has an infection that can respond to an antibiotic, it should be used. If people choose to use a homeopathic approach and it works, that's fine, as long as the people who prescribe it or ascribe to it recognize its limitations.

We take all precautions, but what do I do if my baby should pull herself up on a hot stove and burn herself?

Use ice, not butter. Even better, immerse her hand in cold water instead of applying ice. Then get down to the emergency room, where proper treatment can be prescribed, and that's usually a salve called Silvadene, which protects the skin.

#356 *Do you treat scalding the same as a burn?*

Yes, here again, cold is the proper treatment. However, scalding frequently results in more severe burns because of the layers of skin affected and the larger area the hot water can cover. The emergency room doctors will determine if the baby needs to be taken to a burn center. That's why you just can't be too careful with hot water when there's a baby around.

REMINDER: Hot water burns. ALWAYS test the bath water before immersing an infant, a toddler or a child.

#357 *My baby is now on solid food, but he absolutely refuses to eat any vegetables at all. Is this a terrible thing?*

Not at all. This is temporary. Someday, he's going to choose to eat vegetables on his own, so don't worry about it at all.

#358 *Now he eats only one thing—chicken noodle dinner—every single day. He just won't take anything else. What can I do?*

Nothing. You can continue to offer him new things, but if he likes chicken noodle and it's a healthy dinner, it's okay for him to eat it every day. At some point, he'll tire of it and try new foods. They all do.

Anyway, forcing food on a baby is almost never successful and may actually contribute to an eating disorder later on.

What do I do if he spits up some blood?

If you are breast-feeding and you have a small crack in the nipple, he may get a little blood in his mouth and spit it back up. If he's a crawler and he spits up blood, it may mean that he's bumped his lip and, because the mouth bleeds so profusely, he's swallowed some blood and it's come back up. If it is bright red blood, the chances are that it's coming from his nose, not his stomach, and it will stop on its own. All of these things are possible; none is serious.

#360

Can you freeze breast milk for future use?

Yes, it's a great idea to freeze breast milk. It can stay in the freezer up to six months without a problem.

#361

At what point does a baby understand language?

Learning a language, as we all know, is an ongoing process, and the level of comprehension increases with the amount of exposure as well as with maturity. Very small babies, while they may not understand the words you use, understand your tone of voice and your body language. He learns by your tone what no means. And, if you raise both arms and say "Touchdown!" often enough, your baby will eventually put up his arms, too, when he hears the word. Then when you react with delighted applause, he, too, is delighted and will continue to respond this way. Even the most proud parent will acknowledge that the baby doesn't really know the meaning of the word touchdown. However, as he grows, his little brain is like a sponge, soaking up all this new information at an amazing rate. And when he begins to talk, you can be sure he knows the meaning of the word no!

#362 *My ten-month-old said his first word and it's unprintable. I'm afraid it's my fault, but what can I do now?*

Not a damned thing. Seriously, your baby will learn to talk from hearing *you* talk. If there are some words you'd prefer him not to use, do your best not to use those words in his presence. At 10 months old, he's not going to understand the propriety of using certain words, so telling him no will never work. He's just trying out new things, repeating what he's heard. If he stops hearing those words, he'll stop using those words—at that age, anyway.

When is it safe to fly with a baby?

Right away. As you know, I'd rather the baby not be taken into crowds during the first three weeks. However, if it becomes *necessary* for you to fly even in the first few days, it's okay to take the baby. But remember, because the change in air pressure may hurt the baby's ears, make sure he's sucking on something—a pacifier or a bottle—during take-off and landing.

How can I help my toddler get involved with the baby?

Let the toddler "read" a story to the baby. Let him tell a story to the baby. Have the toddler share *his* day, what *he's* done, something he's made in preschool, perhaps, with the baby. Let him hold the baby, take pictures with the baby, play music for the baby, sing to the baby, help you hold the bottle when you feed the baby. He'll get a real kick out of it, especially when the baby is old enough to respond to his big brother or sister with smiles and giggles.

Then again, if he strongly chooses not to get involved with the baby, it may be because he finds his new sibling boring, or he has been spit on or peed on, or most probably has his own, more "interesting" peers to play with.

My baby's almost a year old and I still don't feel as if I've totally bonded. Everything is such a chore. Am I lacking maternal instinct, or what? Am I just not cut out for this?

Some people are born to be mothers. Others are born to feel passionately about some other experiences in their lives. Both types of people become mothers. I've heard it described often as "not bonding enough with the baby." I must say that bonding does not necessarily make a great mother, and that the lack of this bonding—or whatever it is—does not make a bad mother. There's more to being a good parent than bonding. Much more.

I don't think love and bonding necessarily go together, nor is one necessarily the result of the other. I think you have to be patient because love comes with time, and sharing experiences with the growing infant will help you to bond. "Bonding" is just a word. You know, 20 years ago, no one asked about bonding—now, everywhere I speak, I'm asked, "How do you feel about bonding?"

New parenthood is so overwhelming that I have this discussion with many, many new parents. Most new parents do feel terribly inadequate at some point during the first year. This feeling *will* pass. It *does* get better. It *does* get easier.

And no matter which category of parents you fall into, just try to make intelligent, informed choices *most* of the time, and you'll have the most rewarding experience of your lives.